A BRIEF .

ALAN PAINE

A BRIEF LOOK AT LIFE

Copyright © 2008 Alan Paine

The moral right of the author has been asserted.

Apart from any fair dealing for the purposes of research or private study, or criticism or review, as permitted under the Copyright, Designs and Patents Act 1988, this publication may only be reproduced, stored or transmitted, in any form or by any means, with the prior permission in writing of the publishers, or in the case of reprographic reproduction in accordance with the terms of licences issued by the Copyright Licensing Agency. Enquiries concerning reproduction outside those terms should be sent to the publishers.

Matador
9 De Montfort Mews
Leicester LE1 7FW, UK
Tel: (+44) 116 255 9311 / 9312
Email: books@troubador.co.uk
Web: www.troubador.co.uk/matador

ISBN 978-1906221-614

Cover picture from original artwork by artist Richard Bizley, depicting stromatolites, dome shaped structures which he describes as one of the earliest life forms to appear, in shallow seas on Earth over three billion years ago and responsible for creating the Earth's oxygen.

Typeset in 11.5pt Times by Troubador Publishing Ltd, Leicester, UK

Matador is an imprint of Troubador Publishing Ltd

*This book is dedicated to the memory
of my dear daughter Frances
who knew only a brief four years
of that precious commodity we call Life*

CONTENTS

1. Introduction   1
   A new look at some old questions

2. Life and consiousness   7
   What are they and who are we?

3. The human brain   15
   An incredible personal thinking machine

4. Human intelligence   27
   And who is qualified to measure it?

5. The human body   31
   Can it continue to adapt?

6. The Scientific View   37
   The limits of our understanding

---

7. A theological view   49
   The origins of religious belief

8. Religions of the world   55
   Is there any prospect of consensus?

9. Problems with belief   59
   Fragility of Faith

10. Rational Alternatives   63
    Is there another way to know God?

11. Secular morality   67
Across an uncharted sea without a pilot

---

12. The human predicament   73
Our need for a guiding light

13. Economics of human survival   79
The real cost of living

14. Criteria for human and planetary survival   87
Is it already too late

15. Conflict and religious division   95
A tragic waste of human resources

16. Innocence and Guilt   113
Are we all victims of our own ignorance?

---

17. Human achievements   119
Looking on the bright side

18. The future   125
Where do we go from here?

19. Conclusion   131
The beginning of tomorrow's world

The winds of time   133
Index   135
More detailed reading   143

FOREWORD

In this wide ranging survey of the human predicament the author gives his personal view of the phenomena of life and its habitat, and of the theories of some scientists and philosophers, and of some of those authorities' uneasy relationship with theology.

He considers the most basic questions of human identity and the search for the brain's centre of consciousness, and the quest for the far more elusive location of 'self'- the inner spectator that sees and hears and feels and makes decisions, and asks how we have come to experience so much pleasure from some art forms, especially those of colour and music. He contemplates the practical implications of current theories about our universe and our presence in it, and of the incredible physical processes that appear to function in all matter, but reminds us that many of the most fundamental questions still remain to be answered.

He also looks at how the lives of different parts of the human race have been influenced by their varied environments, both political and economic, including those who are fortunate enough to benefit from new scientific advances, and those poverty and disease stricken masses who still lack even the most basic resources. He examines the causes of conflict and asks whether we shall ever emerge from the darkness of racial intolerance and religious contradictions into the daylight of reason.

And how much longer can our home planet, on which all known life depends, continue to support us as we irresponsibly consume tomorrow's finite Earth resources in order to satisfy today's extravagant demands.

1. INTRODUCTION

A new look at some old questions

Anyone attempting to produce a rational view of the incredible phenomenon of life, its origins and its evolution, and to contemplate the possibility that other dimensions may exist of that which we currently perceive to be reality, must inevitably start by wondering whether they can ever hope to write anything new on the subject. Surely by now, everything that could possibly be said has already been published

But although there have been, and are today, many brilliant and highly qualified specialists and writers in this field, not all of them in agreement, most concede that many of the major scientific questions are yet to be answered. It is all too easy to be swayed by the latest scientific and philosophical theories into thinking that we have solved every question that matters, and to forget that the very fundamental bases of our existence on this planet are just as much a mystery as they ever were.

Over forty years ago, in an ever hopeful search for the meaning of everything, I came across the work of someone who seemed to have given more attention than most to the matter. He was a certain Professor Macneile Dixon, who addressed a series of lectures in Glasgow in 1935-7. His command of the English language, and the precision of his use of it, made his written version – 'The Human Situation' both a pleasure to read and an education in itself. But having read – and occasionally re-read, sections of it in more recent years, together with the works of many others who have tried to find some explanation for the universe and our existence in it, I have increasingly found the need to clarify those outstanding questions.

Such was the complexity and detail of Professor Macneile Dixon's lectures, that any attempt to summarise them would be impossible. But clearly he saw the human race at the time as emerging into a new world of clear thinking, unfettered by the restraints of racial intolerance and religious doctrines, and ready to benefit from new scientific discoveries. Yet a couple of years later, in 1939, we were plunged into a second world war that seemed to be sending us back once more into the dark ages.

But it was his main preoccupation with the incredible fact of life itself, and the various ways that humans have responded to their unsought participation in it, that has most exercised my mind. Cause enough to want to start at the beginning and try to put my own observations about this world in some sort of order. How much of what has been told us can we trust?

The first difficulty is that we do not know who or what we are. Most of us – we call ourselves human and like to think we are intellectually superior to all the other creatures on the planet, only partially comprehend our position in time and space. All we know is that we find ourselves looking out through the eyes of living bodies, part of a community of physically similar animals existing, together with many other forms of life, on a rotating sphere of accumulated matter held in almost empty space by forces we do not understand. We have been told, by many highly respected authorities, about our tiny planet's relation to our solar system, that system's place in our galaxy and our galaxy's place as only one of thousands of others in the universe. It is not easy to comprehend the real significance of that, or even of our brief evolution when set against the estimated 4,500 million year time-scale of our world.

In trying to understand all this I have little option at

present but to accept the scientists' observations. My chances of carrying out more than an occasional personal verification are minimal. So I must go along with their planetary hypothesis – it seems reasonable. The stars do move as they say – the planets likewise. The Earth and its moon are there for me to see – they have done their homework. But I must always keep an open mind on the subject – there may yet be other explanations.

They have told us about their understanding of the nature of life and its physical evolution, and how life became possible only because our planet's rotation had minimised extremes of temperature. We are also told about the development of the brain as a control centre helping each animal to avoid danger and maintain itself, and how at some point in time the brains of humans developed to a stage where they gradually began to contemplate their own existence and to ask questions about their environment and their place in it. It all seems very logical.

So in the following pages I want to consider the human predicament, starting by trying to define Life and Consciousness, and to question the multiplicity of explanations which humans have for their origins, for the evolution of their religions and for their widely held belief in the existence of some kind of all powerful and benevolent being called God. What credence can we give to the scientific interpretations of Life and the Universe? Can the creative arts give a deeper meaning to human evolution or are they merely an accidental side effect of brain function? Will the complex machines and structures of our age become our salvation, or merely the rusting memorials of yet another brief civilisation?

I also want to look again at some of those fundamental scientific explanations which, to my mind at least, rely on unsatisfactory assumptions, and at the mosaic of interrelated phenomena that forms the backdrop to our everyday lives.

Surely by now, with our vastly increased scientific knowledge, we can at least eliminate some of the more extreme doctrines that have diverted us from rational thought. It is time for the layman to come forward and ask what all these discoveries and theories, and the laws which the structure of the universe appears to obey, mean for us all in practical terms.

These essays are not intended to compete with any of the vast and stimulating philosophical and scientific literature that already exists, even if I were competent to do so. They are more an effort to extract from it all some basic certainties, if there are any, and to highlight the known uncertainties, of which there are many.

But one thing is certain. In spite of all their magnificent attempts, none of the great philosophers and scientists have yet succeeded in breaching the seemingly impregnable fortress of ultimate knowledge. Its inscrutable facade continues to deny us the truth about our identity and our place in eternity and infinity. Its great doors remain firmly closed.

And what have we done with this gift of life? Is there any clear way forward that will ensure our survival and that of all the other life forms on this planet. Somehow we seem to have created a wilderness of uncontrollable competing interests – an apparently insolvable mess which, coupled with extravagant exploitation of our planet's resources, could even ultimately result in our becoming just one more addition to the long list of extinct civilizations.

Have we any real choice about our ultimate destiny? Are our brains hard wired so that we can never overcome our competitive instincts? Can we ever emerge from the primitive trappings of our ancestry and shake off all the outdated beliefs and conventions that hold us back from acknowledging our ignorance of the true reality of our existence? Can we match our major achievements in science, technology and medicine, with a similar effort to understand ourselves, and perhaps in the process be better able to focus on the root causes of our tiny world's human problems?

Once again the eternal questions, that many philosophers have been asking throughout the ages, and are always hoping one day to find the answers. 'Who are we, what are we doing here, and what is this thing called Life?'

2. LIFE AND CONSCIOUSNESS

What are they, and who are we?

Life? It seems to have appeared on our planet about four billion years ago. But from where? We all seem to have some of it – and, in varying degrees, so do all the other creatures and plants on this planet. But defining it is another matter. What is the difference between say a lump of rock and a piece of wood. The latter surely has that additional feature of having evolved through a process of reproduction. Somehow certain kinds of molecular matter have acquired the capability to interact with each other, make copies of themselves, and combine to form sustainable structures. Although we cannot easily dismiss the rock – it too may include the remains of what had previously been reproductive matter.

Until we can know what drives that reproductive process, what hope is there of going on to understand its evolution through all the stages from basic matter to complex animals such as ourselves, where we have even acquired the ability to question our origins and have developed the capacity for self awareness.

Consider life's various forms:-

1. Bacterial life – why all this vigorous and sometime unwanted (by humans) activity, presumably without any apparent consciousness.

2. Plant life – living organisms without locomotive power, from the most basic, such as lichen, a kind of flowerless combination of algae and fungus, to the massive trees and incredibly complex flowering shrubs. Why do plants try to survive if they have no consciousness? What is it that makes them so persistent in staying alive and perpetuating themselves, e.g. by pollination or seed production?

3. Plant-like creatures such as Zoophytes e.g.: sea anemone.

4. Urchinus – creature inhabiting prickly shell e.g.: sea urchin.

5. Insects – some degree of intelligence, but largely confined to a limited range of mostly instinctive activities.

6. Animal non-human life – a large range of intelligence from small rodents, birds and fish, to the great elephants and whales. Almost all have a herding instinct and some degree of awareness of their surroundings, plus instinctive self preservation and protection of their territory and offspring.

7. Human animals – we consider ourselves to be the most intelligent creatures on the planet, having varying degrees of self awareness plus greater manual and language capability, and even the ability to question our very existence. But why do we want to stay alive and to reproduce? If death is our unavoidable destiny why bother to constantly try to defer it? Would we want to enjoy a particular activity – say a pleasant holiday – if the moment it is finished we have no recollection of it. Surely life is just that – it all ends in nothing, unless of course we accept some religions' promises of an after-life, or that part of us lives on in our children. But perhaps the religions have got it right and we may continue to exist in some other dimension beyond our comprehension.

I am finishing the list with human animals, though the latter's somewhat conceited assumption could be challenged on the grounds that we are thinking only of a human type of intelligence, as our understanding of say a dolphin's brain activity is insufficient. And is language the only means of communication? How does a flock of birds change direction with such unity – without any apparent leader? And when diving near a vast shoal of tiny fish I have often wondered how they can all instantly change direction. Who is the boss there? Could there be some kind of collective Id, a means of communication superior to our own. We may yet find that we are not so smart after all !

So what is Life? It could be described as the ability of otherwise inactive materials to chemically interact with each other and reproduce themselves. But it seems that somehow the existence of conscious life, that is the ability of creatures to be aware of their presence in, and to respond to, their environment, is additional to their physical state. Almost as if it is something totally separate and invisible, which needs a reproductive animal medium in order to see, hear and feel, the physical world. I do not find it difficult to accept that when we are born we each inherit, from one or both of our parents, a copy of this mysterious life force. We have all experienced that gradual dawning awareness of our own sense of being as we begin to receive, recognise and ultimately understand, sound, tactile and visual stimulation from the world about us. But we are none the wiser in our attempts to contain conscious life in some sort of scientific package – to describe it in technical terms.

One problem with defining consciousness is that there are many degrees of it. Some creatures may be aware of danger and react instinctively to it without having the ability to consider various options for improving their long term survival. Their consciousness is limited to immediate needs rather than to the contemplation of their own predicament and to plan ahead. But what kind of consciousness has a squirrel? It can plan ahead to stock nuts for winter survival and even think of ingenious ways to gain access to food not intended for it. It has good manual dexterity, so what has stopped it from more constructive activities? Probably it has no need, or awareness of need, for a more sophisticated lifestyle and consequently no stimulus to develop new ideas. And its consciousness may not include an ability to wonder about its environment or to contemplate the stars. On the other hand evolution is a slow process, so its development might not necessarily be apparent to us and they could still evolve further in time.

So how does human consciousness differ. Certainly we, or at least some of us, will give thought to our place in the world, or even in the universe. We plan our lives in order to acquire the best future for ourselves and our children and sometimes devote our efforts to the benefit of our wider community. But we can also look inwards and contemplate our own existence – dwell at length on all the mysteries of Life and the Universe – make complex judgements about the relative merits of this or that course of action – be happy or sad. This is the extra degree of self awareness – the inner personality, which looks out from inside our own minds, yet can also look inwards into the inner sanctum of our own reasoning processes – to challenge our own judgement – to ask 'who am I' – 'why am I here' – 'I do not remember my beginning'- 'will I one day cease to be'? This is the real stuff of consciousness, but there are many different levels of it, and not all humans necessarily think deeply enough, and some are not intelligent enough, to even be aware of their potential capabilities to the same degree.

I think we first have to ask ourselves why we all have the stimulus to stay alive. Something seems to have been instilled in all life forms that makes them fear, or at least resist, death and take the most rewarding course of action to stay alive and reproduce. Could that built in stimuli, contained in our genes, give us the extra ingredient of conscious self awareness. It does not appear to function in what we call the lower forms of life – they still have the urge to stay alive and reproduce, but do not appear to possess the emotions we attribute to ourselves. That elusive self consciousness seems to exist in another dimension altogether – some sort of independent medium coexisting with the human brain.

And apart from how life started, on our planet and elsewhere, there is also the question of whether there is any kind of continuing existence for each of us after death has deprived us of a physical presence. If we survive to old age, some of us will begin to lose that precious personality and no longer even know ourselves. Where has that personality gone? Has it just dissolved away, or has it somehow deserted its host body and passed into some other form of existence beyond our comprehension.

One of the reasons why some of us are inclined to doubt the possibility of any kind of on-going experience after death has been that we cannot envisage any way in which we could see without eyes or hear without ears or experience any other kind of sense in the absence of the necessary physical apparatus to acquire such information. But recently I have pondered on the process of dreaming, where we see, and hear, in our sleep, sights and sounds generated within our own brains. In that process we are not receiving external information, at least not through our acknowledged senses, but the sights and sounds are nonetheless being experienced without the concurrent use of eyes and ears, even though both senses have played a part on some previous occasions in our lives, creating the library of images and sounds which we draw upon to dream.

So is it possible that, when we die, our inner self, the Id, could somehow be transposed into some other dimension and be receiving data through an alternative receiving device – one that exists in a different medium altogether? After all, what our eyes normally 'see' is instantly converted into electrochemical impulses which our brains then analyse. Could there perhaps be other ways of receiving data that would convey equally accurate information. But this mysterious Id has arisen only after our birth, unless it has been inherited from our parents, so perhaps, unless we have children, we shall just cease to exist one day.

But consider the incredible but invisible activity in the space around us. Even in a small room, in the air, even passing through our own heads, billions of transmissions from radio, television, mobile phones, gravity, various magnetic fields, all without us being aware of them, until and unless we decide to use our television or radio or mobile phone to access some of it, and even then only that bit of it which we require. So with all that going on why should we find it difficult to imagine that, after we die, we could continue to exist, and in some equally undetectable medium still be aware of the sights and sounds that we are currently able to receive?

There is no end to the number of questions we can ask about our identity and the incredible world in which we find ourselves. But how about the apparatus we each possess that enables us to be aware of our situation and to formulate those questions. If you or I can, in a fraction of a second, receive an instant picture of our surroundings, updated twenty-five times a second, what does this say for the processing capacity of the human brain. It is indeed an unbelievably complex and powerful machine, which seems to be able to function without interference from all those billions of electromagnetic transmissions constantly passing through it. Yet it is only at the very beginning in its efforts to understand itself.

Perhaps we should approach this question from another direction, and consider the human brain itself, and try to find out in what part of it this elusive consciousness, and even the centre of self awareness, resides.

3. THE HUMAN BRAIN

An incredible personal thinking machine

Most modern personal computers have an astonishing processing rate. Mine (circa 2003) is apparently capable of 10 million calculations per second. The average television set can review 250,000 dots 25 times per second, or over 6,000,000 pieces of information. But the human brain appears to be able to deal with far more than this, absorbing incoming information from an area at least a hundred times the size of a TV screen, or more than 600 million changes per second. Even allowing for the extremities of peripheral vision being limited in detail and alerted only by the detection of movement, the sheer magnitude of the brain's capacity puts the man-made devices in their place.

Visual information however, accounts for only a small part of the brain's activity. Add to that the sound and tactile senses and then consider the even more remarkable ability to process all this detail. We have to act immediately in some cases, to avoid danger for instance, while much other information is rapidly sifted, analysed, compared with existing knowledge and used to supplement it. All our actions depend on our brain's ability to judge that complex mass of acquired information. A good example is found in the process of driving a car along a busy road, where a multitude of rapidly changing situations have to be taken into account. Other vehicles, pedestrians, sudden unexpected movements of children or dogs, various obstructions, all to be anticipated and much of it automatically dealt with while we are possibly also thinking about our destination and planning the route for the rest of our journey.

But something far more complex is going on than the mere processing of information, however incredible that mechanism may seem. Somewhere deep inside each of us lies the inner person, the centre or HQ from whence we look out onto the world about us. The Id – where the unique individual resides, the personality that contains those ongoing elements from our parents', and their parents', personalities right back to the dawn of life on earth, and which is subsequently expanded by experiences during our own lives. This is the inner sanctum where we know pleasure and pain, joy and sadness, and make those more difficult decisions which cannot be left to our automatic reflexes to decide. But where in the human brain does this inner sanctum reside? We cannot identify any one part as each seems to perform a different function, yet it is difficult to imagine the whole brain functioning without some kind of co-ordinating centre.

We have to begin somewhere. In the past few decades we have become able to use, often without fully understanding the process, an incredible array of electronic devices. I hesitate to refer to 'electronic brains', but they are able to collect, store and process billions of items of data and to do it in ever smaller assemblies of inter-relating components. Every time we think we cannot devise anything smaller to do our calculating, someone manages yet another quantum shrinkage.

If we look at the brain as a kind of computer, able to receive information and respond mechanically with appropriate action, then surely it becomes just a matter of how sophisticated are its circuits. For example if our computer receives visual information from a video camera, say it is a security device, and it has observed someone carrying out a particular action, then it can be programmed to consult its memory to decide whether that action is criminal and if so both record the event and alert a responsible authority. So in that case it is doing what a human brain could do and if we have designed the computer we will know the location of its co-ordinating centre. We could further enhance our computer's capability by adding a voice recognition device. Current versions simply hear words and print them without any requirement to understand them. But assuming it could be programmed to recognise the meaning of words and sentences, then once more it could respond with appropriate action, and even reply verbally. So far no insurmountable difficulty – it would be able to see and hear, recognise objects and faces, assess the need for a response and, if required, take action including speech.

Have we already the equivalent of a human brain, albeit that of a comparatively simple person? Could it in time, given a substantial memory bank, come to develop human characteristics? It would need to be able to judge the merits of each possible course of action, but could it include the ability to consider moral issues and develop sensitivities to human emotional expression? These last two characteristics might be very difficult to emulate. We would need to understand how the brain makes a judgement on whether a course of action is right or wrong. And we all know that humans can make mistakes. We might wake up one morning feeling unwell and make a response to some event that we would later decide had been wrong.

There have been many attempts to produce machines with something resembling intelligence, and the ever increasing sophistication of electronic computers, even if not yet successful in fully emulating human mental processes, has at least given us a much greater insight into the complexity of those processes in our own brains. The basic prerequisites for replicating a conscious life form could be summarised as follows:

a) a machine with the ability to respond electronically or mechanically to a given stimulus, be it sound, visual or tactile.

b) an ability to recognise, from a built in memory, a set of circumstances which would require it to respond.

c) the ability to anticipate, from its accumulated knowledge, what may happen in the near future, and take preparatory action.

The third prerequisite is of course the most difficult of the three to emulate, and would depend on the anticipated causative input. If for example its memory told it that, in ten minutes time, it would have to make a specific sound – no problem – my alarm clock already has that capability. But if it had to consider probabilities, and make rational choices between several options, that is a different matter. The way our brains do this depends very much on acquired experience, and we do sometimes make mistakes.

So are we saying that the human brain could be replicated by a computerised machine providing we give that machine sufficient memory and circuitry to enable it to make comparative evaluations? Its memory would of course have to be loaded with details of every possible type of situation, and include some kind of weighting factor reflecting the relative importance of each one. It would also need the ability to learn from each event and so update and improve its subsequent performance. Perhaps our theoretical machine could do better than a human brain. It would not be hampered by the kind of distractions that we have from our bodies' variable chemistry and nervous systems.

But better in what way. The basic purpose of our brain is

to maintain our body's ability to survive. As a supplement to that process the machine could be useful, but otherwise it is essentially a memory resource with the installed ability to process supplied information and respond. Suppose we programme it to react to a threat to its own survival. How would we make it 'care' about itself? Even if we present it with the ability to recognise say a computer virus as being a threat to its central processor and to respond to that threat by disarming it, our machine does not intrinsically care if it ceases to function, in the same way that a human may care.

So there has to be a fourth prerequisite d) self awareness. This is the extra sense that makes us human. Can we produce a machine that is capable of feeling sad, or happy, or desires more satisfying input. One perhaps that feels aggressive, or desires to please. What kinds of reward would it need to make it try to do better? Without such stimuli, that we all need to preserve our health and get satisfaction out of life, our computerised machine will neither demand, nor respond to, such encouragement.

Is this 'care' aspect the essential 'self' that we are looking for, that distinguishes us from the machine. A built in survival device that we cannot replicate? Even if the machine might come to develop a degree of self awareness in the same way that a child gradually acquires it, in the end it would have no more reason to care for its own survival than a person contemplating suicide.

Are we any nearer to finding the human brain's control centre or 'HQ' where the 'self' resides? We appear to be looking for a kind of central processor that has as its prime function the health and wellbeing of its supporting physical body. It could instinctively include intellectual activities if greater understanding of its environment were perceived to be beneficial. And we know which parts of the brain are responsible for most mental and body functions, and it is possible that the elusive control centre is resident somewhere in the cerebral cortex, the outer region where we appear to do most of our thinking, together with the visual cortex where images are processed. Are we there yet? No, I think not. It is difficult to imagine this control centre, wherever it lies in the brain, as being somehow able to know itself. Some scientists in recent years have come to the conclusion that we are just a bundle of very clever neurons. Many others though remain unconvinced. A few even suspect that the very nature of the process of self contemplating self means that we can never know the ultimate significance of being.

But there are other aspects of consciousness that currently seem to defy understanding. Not only can most of us hear and see the world about us. Some sounds and sights also give us pleasure or displeasure. How do our brains, or at least some brains, come to have this appreciation of things pleasant or unpleasant – the beautiful or the ugly – and the various art forms which we use to illustrate them.

Music for example is an art form that seems to function at the deepest level of brain awareness, and can both inspire and complement most of the others. But there is a limit to which any particular art form can be understood in isolation. They all belong to a kind of totality, a means of describing any combination of events which unite to form a balanced and satisfying whole. The hind leg of an antelope for example can be described as beautiful, its movement as graceful, but to the biologist or the engineer its structure is an elegant physical perfection in which bone and muscle are used in the most economical way, a compromise between strength and minimum weight. So we could say, in that case at least, that when we find something to be artistically satisfying, we are simply responding to an instinctive appreciation of what is structurally perfect.

Can we apply this principle in other ways. How did music evolve from its primitive rhythmic origins? Could this art form be a 'side effect' of the way in which the human brain operates. Why do we recognise harmonic structure? Why do we recognise for instance, without the need to know why, the relationship between middle C and C an octave lower? Somehow our brains are tuned to the fact that the former is vibrating at exactly twice the number of cycles per second than the latter. And why is harmonic sound pleasant and discord unpleasant? Why does a cadence bring a sense of relief, a sense of having arrived, while its absence leaves us hanging in mid-air waiting for it. Now it is hard to imagine that the brain has evolved that way solely to be able to appreciate music. It must have some other function, something more fundamental to our, and perhaps other creatures', survival.

Brain memory and processing functions may be the key. It could be that the mental sorting process is split into many levels of incoming data recording. There is an initial need to dump within a few seconds perhaps ninety -nine per cent of all incoming information. The other one percent being saved into the next level which is again reduced by ninety-nine per cent and so on. But each level involves a more refined elimination process until we get to the highest level where long term memory is stored. Could it be that each bit of information requires a comparison process to find out if it has been seen before. If it is recognised then it supplements what is already there. If its predecessor has already gone to a higher level then that level of memory also needs to be searched until the new data can take its appropriate place.

The key to the music question might be that each level of memory is related mathematically, being a precise multiple, or reduction, in cycles per second over its predecessor. Somehow sonic vibrations impinge directly on this layered structure, and the purer their harmonic properties the easier it is for the brain to recognise them and the greater is the resulting pleasure. Conversely of course a discord requires an unrewarding search and produces displeasure.

Somewhere in this direction we will find an explanation for the uplifting effects of the major chords and the depression of the minor, and all the other joy and sadness, triumph and despair that we now associate with this direct intrusion into the deeper levels of consciousness.

This ability to associate music and rhythmic activity has been with us since earliest times, from aboriginal war dances to trumpet calls announcing great events or summons to battle. But we now have a vast accumulation of classic and contemporary music which we can enjoy and use to accompany and enhance stage and film drama. And in ballet and other dance forms we often see a combination of music and dramatic movement set against a scenic backdrop. Walt Disney, in his 1945 film 'Fantasia' created, with the aid of eight very different pieces of classical music, a remarkable combination of music with abstract and partly animated scenery. And perhaps one of the greatest examples of musically inspired emotion is Wagner's evocative Love Duet in his 1865 opera Tristan and Isolde, with its gradual rhythmic rise in excitement, its ultimate orgasmic crescendo and subsequent quiet reflective calm. It seems that, in the same way that our nervous systems can be stimulated by drinking wine, or by taking certain drugs, they can likewise be stimulated by hearing particular combinations of sound frequencies.

So what of the purely graphic arts. Can we find scientific explanations for their emotional appeal? Form, shape, depth and perspective seem to satisfy in many ways. But some reasons are hard to find. Form and shape as I said earlier owe much to the demands of nature for strength and economy in structure, and we therefore find pleasure in anything that expresses that ideal. Yet deliberate deviation also seems to satisfy on occasion, providing it is consistent, when for instance it is trying to enhance the gross or the delicate nature of the subject. True perspective satisfies for its obvious capability to express reality, but can be inappropriate if the subject itself is enhanced or exaggerated. Colour is a major factor enabling many animals, including most of us, to identify vital characteristics of other creatures and objects, friendly or otherwise. Bright yellow usually means warm sunshine, red is associated with fire, but also with blood and danger. Blue (feeling blue?) with cold and depression. Green with freshness and living, black with death and not a major presence in pictorial art. But the pure joy of multiple colours probably, as with music, owes its effect to the way in which the brain stores information, and combinations that most please us are possibly those which, in wavelength terms, have an harmonic relationship.

So have we arrived at a possible explanation for our brains' ability to obtain pleasure or displeasure from some sounds and visions? Is there more to it than that? Why have our emotions become so involved? Could it be that sounds which our ancestors regarded as pleasant, such as bird songs, were associated with security and the absence of danger, while other sights and sounds, such as a thunderstorm or the trumpeting of an elephant, excited or alarmed them? And why do we raise the pitch of our voices when we are excited or in pain?

Our emotions seem to be influenced by many factors, not all of them rationally explicable. They appear to involve more than just physical comfort or discomfort. What about love – this often tormenting condition can mean different things to each of us. It can be just physical desire – it can be entirely compassionate – it can be varying degrees of both. It can even be simply a desire to be loved.

Then we come to sadness and despair – again with physical effects. When someone close to us dies, surely something more than physical inconvenience is making us sad? To cry – to feel physically ill with grief. The inner self – which we thought we had prepared to cope with the outside world, has suddenly become disrupted by external events for which we were not prepared. And a degree of this sadness has been observed in some other animals, with the loss of a mate for instance.

There are also physical components to emotional events. Nervously induced chemical responses in the body, probably related to fear or anticipation or impending competitive action – that sudden feeling in the pit of the stomach for instance – the blush of embarrassment – the rise in blood pressure even though we could be unaware of it.

Yet here again the subconscious has a great deal to do with it. Could emotions be driven by experiences of the outcomes of a lifetime of past events, such that while much of the detail of those events has been long forgotten, there remains a kind of subconscious accumulation of basic preferences – simply concluding that a certain happening is desirable or otherwise without necessarily being able to self analyse to know why? And there are also inherited factors including physical desires, which can function in the subconscious to influence decisions.

Surely we have now identified the personality – it has been hiding all along inside the subconscious – the self – elusive because we cannot, at any one moment, be conscious of all the events in our lives which have together contributed to our decision making capability. Neither can we necessarily be fully aware of our personal physical driving forces, which have contributed to our present attitude to life and to those around us. Our responses are largely instinctive and drawn from the inner sanctum, which may resist change. But can we always rely on our reasoning apparatus to make the right decision? What happens for example when someone finds one day that their life has become intolerable, perhaps through illness or grief or they feel that it is no longer worth living? They might at the time even be contemplating suicide. But a week later their subconscious might give them a different view and all is well again. In spite of our imagined self control, there seems to be no totally reliable final arbiter hiding in this inner sanctum. External events and the body's own variable chemistry all affect the outcome.

And while we might have found a location for self, it could be argued that it does not necessarily bring us much nearer to understanding self awareness. Surely we have still not identified the inner person – the spectator that uses the apparatus of self.

Could it be that self awareness is something that simply evolves in each of us as we develop from childhood, a kind of awakening. It may be that its existence is simply the outcome of the gradual emergence of increasing degrees of consciousness from the initial instincts we have at birth. The acquisition of consciousness, and ultimately self-awareness, is a gradual process. Even so, for the purpose of understanding this we could think of it as a series of stages:

a) Baby being fed by mother – drinks instinctively.
b) Recognises mother – anticipates food and comfort.
c) Learns that crying brings food and comfort.
d) Develops an ability to use crying to get its own way.
e) Learns to reach out and obtain things for itself.
f) Learns to talk and ask for things.
g) Becomes selective and expresses preferences
h) Learns that some experiences can be painful and develops fear.
i) Learns to ask questions.
j) Becomes resentful of criticism.
k) Becomes aware of sexuality and desires.
l) Begins to wonder and asks where they came from.
m) Becomes dissatisfied with some of the answers.
n) Experiences illness and unhappiness.
o) Questions their own mistakes -where did they go wrong?

p) Develops a degree of introspection and/or extroversion.
q) Develops awareness of self, if not achieved at an earlier stage.
r) Recognises that it has that self awareness.

It could therefore be argued that self awareness can arise at almost any stage, depending perhaps on the degree of a persons' inherited intelligence, but would probably appear not much earlier than stage 'j', as a result of criticism. Stage 'n' illness or unhappiness could certainly evoke some degree of inward contemplation. It might of course never appear, even in a very intelligent person, if they have an entirely extrovert personality and have never experienced deep unhappiness or serious illness, but such a person might lack the sensitivity to others' needs which would normally come from inner experience.

So a new born child could advance gradually, from the initial entirely automatic responses, through all those stages, until it has grown sufficiently to develop self awareness, and has recognised that it has that self awareness. Perhaps that is all there is to it. We are not born with self awareness and most of us will lose some of it in our final years.

This writer is not entirely convinced by his own arguments, but perhaps he is just unwilling to accept the implications. That we are each the product of our ancestors' experiences. That our consciousness evolves from birth, and our inner self awakens from nothing and after a life of increasing awareness declines to end in nothing. Surely there has to be something more to it all than that. Will we ever know the answer?

But given this glimpse of the possible nature and location of the conscious and self aware personality, can we now try to see how it relates to human intelligence?

4. HUMAN INTELLIGENCE

And who is qualified to measure it?

The paradox of definition of intelligence by contemporary humans, even by those who we regard as having a good measure of it, is that they can only define it within the confines of their own intellectual capacity. So any attempt by myself to do so must acknowledge those same limitations. The Oxford dictionary refers to it simply as 'quickness of understanding' and it is true that standard intelligence tests primarily measure it in terms of the number of accurate answers given in a specified time, the length of time being calculated such that no one individual is expected to complete all the answers in that time. But this definition fails in many ways. It is like a club defining its own membership qualifications – it is like doctors or solicitors sitting on examination boards deciding who qualifies to be doctors or solicitors. We must not forget to question the examiners' qualifications, otherwise we can end up with some inadequate people already at the top of the ladder (and it is inevitable that there always will be) simply helping similarly undeserving candidates up behind them. The definition also fails by setting a time limit on intelligence tests, not because time has no place in the assessment, but it ignores those whose intelligent processes operate in a different way. The deep thinkers of this world should also be allowed to set some of the questions, and allow all the time needed for the candidates to answer them.

But of course this brings me full circle to the paradoxical

question – 'how do we identify the top intelligence in the first place,' since we need someone even higher to both lay down the criteria and place the winner on the throne? And it is surely necessary to consider whether there are variations in intelligence depending on subject matter. A person could be a brilliant mathematician yet be quite dim witted at chemistry, even if they put their mind to it. Do we also have to accept that there is no absolute maximum achievable intelligence? Does it have to be open ended at the top?

How do we start in our effort to find a better overall definition, if there is one? Intelligence appears to have developed as part of the survival mechanism. But there are other components of that mechanism in most creatures. Perhaps the largest is proliferation, where for example most insects or sea creatures each produce thousands of offspring to ensure that at least a few might survive. And humans appear to need thousands of sperm to produce mostly only one child. Then there is the sex process, the almost universal procreation device that seems to be intended to ensure that defective genes are progressively eliminated. But these are all instinctive processes. So we could describe intelligence as the point at which consciousness takes over from instinct.

There are several aspects of intelligence. The first I would describe as Survival based, the second being Prosperity based and the third would be Knowledge. Much overlap of course but I have to start somewhere.

The Survival Aspect: In this case two opposing factors are present. They are Speed of thinking and Depth of thinking. If a creature takes too long to decide on a course of action when danger approaches it may be too late to escape, even if it has thought of a more efficient way of avoiding that danger. Delay can also help the predator to plan its attack more precisely. So I am back to the disputed 'time limit' on intelligence tests. Survival therefore seems to need speed of thinking when under immediate threat and depth for planning ahead. So birds react to every movement or noise by instant flight, but choose their nesting sites with a view to long term security. But is this intelligence, or simply an evolutionary acquired automatic response? And how much of our own 'intelligence' is similarly no more than an inherited series of instinctive reactions? Instinct could be the root or origin of intelligence and the two need to be considered together.

Prosperity aspect: The same two opposing factors are present, but depth is probably the more important. Of course it could still be necessary to make rapid decisions, if you are bidding on the stock exchange for instance, though death is an unlikely consequence of failure to make the right decision. But this kind of activity could require a very broad based understanding of a complex market, and intelligence here would need to be very flexible with an ability to evaluate many subtle inter-reacting components.

Knowledge aspect: While knowledge is to some degree an ingredient of the previous two aspects it can be considered as an intellectual discipline in itself. Speed is usually unimportant here. Obviously intelligence can only function with the material of knowledge and the latter can only be put to good use if we have the intelligence to understand it. But it is the search for understanding, and the ability to relate facts from multiple sources and spot minute clues that would otherwise pass unnoticed, that requires the highest available intelligence. Yet once again a master in the acquisition of knowledge might make a poor showing in say, speed of reaction to danger or a game of chess.

But all three aspects of intelligence can only develop and function effectively if the mental machinery is efficient. The inner self – the subconscious apparatus which we think we have identified, is essential in that it provides the judgement and selectivity, based as we said in the last chapter, not only on our own development from birth but also on our inherited perceptual capabilities.

And can we ever be free of the influence of our ancestors when it comes to making judgements. Surely our reasoning powers – our attitudes – our whole thinking processes, are based on the unique brain structure which we each inherit from our parents and their parents, right back to the dawn of time. Is it possible that, by acknowledging that fact, we could detach from our previously unwitting reliance on it and learn to base our judgements solely on available facts? But facts often need interpretation – that is when our brain's ability to compare and evaluate competing sources of information usually relies on its unique ancestrally biased structure. Consider also the effects of lifetime experience – much of it acquired as the result of chance, depending on which sources of information, and the influence of others, happened to be encountered, especially during early formative years. Those past events, although perhaps long since forgotten, can subconsciously influence our later perceptive capabilities.

Intelligence is not of course to be equated with knowledge, but it is surely the ability to acquire knowledge, interpret it and apply it, rather than 'quickness of understanding'. Could this be a sufficient definition?

All this of course cannot be considered in isolation. Our thinking and decision making machinery cannot exist without the support of a physical human body.

5. THE HUMAN BODY

Can it continue to adapt?

While pondering on the incredible nature of our brains, we cannot ignore our equally incredible supporting physical bodies. The brain cannot function without a constant supply of oxygen, delivered through the blood supply. And that is totally dependent on an elaborate system whereby the blood is continuously being refreshed with oxygen and purified through a multiplicity of organs. Maintaining all that apparatus requires energy, and that is of course obtained by ingesting food and fluid, and breathing air containing oxygen. And finally we have to maintain our ability to reproduce ourselves. Most of the above processes operate automatically, and for the remainder, such as the need for food and fluid, the brain provides an instinctive demand which we ignore at our peril. But our basic instincts can be affected by our current state of mind and, conversely, our state of mind can be very much affected by our state of health. A two way affair, which brings us right back to the question of who is the boss – the brain or the body?

The unity of the brain and body, and the exercise of the former over the latter, will power, raises many questions. But the body itself seems, like most animals, to have become not only a very complicated structure, but to need a large variety of nutrient chemicals to maintain good health. How have we become so dependent on such a critical mix? Surely our more primitive ancestors did not always have the range of food available to them that we consider necessary. Neither would they have realised the need for a balanced diet. Yet many of them survived to procreate, and we are here to prove it. Perhaps it is our long since departure from entirely natural evolutionary processes that has necessitated such complicated adjustments to our diet.

The actual structure of the body, with all its incredibly inter-related organs, again begs the question of how did it all come to be that way. We are told about evolution and how we are supposed to be the product of several hundred million years of adaptation to our environment, but what is the mechanism whereby our systems respond to those influences? If some change occurred – it would have to be gradual – say in the oxygen content of the atmosphere, or in something already of concern to us, such as the reduction in the earth's ozone layer. What part of our brain/body system would stimulate and control our adaptation. Do we even know that we could adapt? Evolution may have its limitations.

Whereas evolutionary processes are the only adaptive devices available to most animals to cope with climate changes, we can construct shelters, cooled or heated as required. We can apply sun cream or wear warmer clothes or take medicinal supplements. The most that other animals can do is to take advantage of natural resources such as sheltering in a cave or migrating, although a few seem instinctively to know the medicinal benefits of certain plants and minerals.

One problem with evolution theory is that we tend to assume that its process is somehow pre-defined, a kind of law with a fixed destination. If that were so then surely our planetary environment would have been included in the original recipe, rather than the reverse, where all our evolution is probably nothing more than an automatic response to it. The human animals' superior manipulative abilities and assumed superior intelligence coupled with being able to communicate by language, have obviously given us a lead in being able to modify certain aspects of our environment, but in the end we may, as I have said earlier, simply destroy everything.

Our adaptations to the world's environment may have been unnatural, but they may nonetheless have been unavoidable. Our ideal climate might be somewhere in Africa or the Mediterranean or the Middle East or Central America or parts of Australia. But for many reasons our ancestors spread out to occupy less hospitable climates. They could not wait for evolution to take its leisurely course. The moment we started to clothe ourselves in animal fur we started to depart from natural evolution. Our survival came to depend on other artificial aids such as caves or latterly houses with some form of heating. And the past century has seen the development of air-conditioning, enabling some of us to live in comfort in otherwise intolerably hot climates.

Surely we have exposed a potential disaster. The warning bells should be sounding. If we go on providing ourselves with ever more external protection rather than adapting our bodies to climate change, we will become less and less prepared to cope with some major natural, or man-made, upheaval that could take away all the artificial supporting structures and energy consuming devices that we currently enjoy. What chance of survival then? And are we just getting even more complex, with still greater risks as we depart from nature's built in automatic selective processes?

But maybe this whole premise is wrong. Perhaps we have not departed from natural evolution after all. These sophisticated inventions and life styles resulting from our assumed superior intelligence are surely no more unnatural than a bird building a nest, or the ants underground tunnels, or a beaver damming a stream. We have simply responded to our habitat and, if we damage or destroy it in the process we are no more outside of nature's random but inefficient selection process than a plague of locusts.

And it is all too easy to assume that evolution is a progressive process where animal life is constantly improving. But there are situations, the ostrich is one example, where its original ability to fly has been lost, presumably because its lifestyle changed such that it no longer found that ability necessary for its survival. Probably its great size, up to eight feet tall, and its high running speed, gave it all the protection it needed from its predators.

But could the human animal also experience retrogressive evolution and lose one or more of its acquired capabilities. One possibility is that our hearing ability could become less discriminatory. How often do most of us find ourselves in an environment where we need to, or even want to, hear the faint sounds of nature, like the rustle of leaves in the wind or faint warning sounds of a potential predator. And in the modern world, where most of us are surrounded by traffic noise or loud radio and television programmes, less and less of us even have our hearing tuned to listen to such things as the quieter parts of classical music. And every year more and more people are having to obtain hearing aids. So that finer aspect of human hearing could be gradually evolving out of use.

Perhaps other aspects of human abilities are pending extinction. Will we, with the advent of so much powered transport, ultimately suffer from a reduced ability to use our own legs. And anyway we rarely have to use our legs these days to escape from predators. Today's enemies are more likely to be bacterial. Certainly there is already a marked increase in obesity in much of so called western civilization, and this alone means that those so affected have reduced mobility. And what about our taste buds. Some still treasure their ability to enjoy the finest wines and the most delicate flavours, but the dominant trend in most of the population seems to be towards strong sauces and bland foods. And our sense of smell, under attack by car exhaust fumes – may still be useful if we wish to appreciate flowers and fine scents, but can we retain it?

So evolution in our case could ultimately produce humans who have lost all those characteristics previously necessary for survival in our original natural environment. But does it matter? Only maybe if we regard the more aesthetic aspects of life as worth keeping, and even then only if a sufficient proportion of the human race participate in maintaining those aspects in the gene bank.

Natural or otherwise, how do we evaluate the human genome project, which has given us a vast new insight into our cell structure and evolution? As we proceed with unravelling the DNA molecular mechanisms we learn more and more about the complex relationship between the cells, giving us greater opportunities to understand and treat diseases. Yet here again are we any nearer knowing why these cells appear to be committed to respond? What drives them? Why and how did evolution evolve?

And what chance have we of fully understanding the most incredible process of all – reproduction? Humans, like all living creatures, have the capability to create copies of themselves, perhaps with some co-operation from the lunar cycle. Consider the male / female combination of DNA information and the resulting subsequent orderly assembly of all the parts needed to produce in most cases a perfect child. In spite of all we know about it, the motivation for all those components to obediently take their allotted places in the growing foetus still leaves much to be explained. Nature's creative capability seems to demonstrate a greater degree of intelligence than that found in any of its life forms.

What do the scientists have to say about the material world in which we find ourselves, and about the chemistry and physical structure of matter and of all living creatures?

6. A SCIENTIFIC VIEW

The limits of our understanding

In the course of the twentieth century there developed a more free thinking approach to scientific research, especially as science gradually diverged from its previous religious constraints. Various disciplines were beginning to recognise the existence of each other and scientists were moving outside their previously strict and precise mathematical and material boundaries, to consider whether there were other interpretations of some of the phenomena that at present lack convincing explanations.

One famous author of the early twentieth century, G.K.Chesterton, in one of his detective novels, portrayed the hero, who was a priest, reflecting on his companions' tendency to confuse cause and effect. Can we be sure, he said to them, when we see trees blowing in the wind, that it is the wind causing the trees to move rather than the trees waving about creating the wind. It is essential that we too look at everything with a similar analytical eye, turning each new piece of information on its head so to speak, to see if it still makes sense, even looking at well established scientific statements about the incredible phenomena of this world to see if we can think of any more acceptable ways to explain them.

Can we be sure of anything about the true nature of our existence? Are we all being manipulated in any way by some external force? Does the rest of the world really exist or is all our experience simply implanted in our minds, like some kind of dream? Do we actually exist elsewhere, and by some remote connection receive information from our bodies and control their actions? When we die and our bodies cease to function will we, on being cut off from all external (physical?) experience, become aware of our true location and identity in time and space?

After all our explorations, our scientific discoveries and our attempts to understand ourselves, do we know anything with any certainty about our origins. Could the whole geological and environmental set up, with its huge variety of creatures and life forms, including the illusion of a vast time-scale, have been much more recently created by some superior intelligence? Could all the apparent fossils, the geological strata and the evidence of the age of everything which we think we have obtained from radio-carbon dating, have been simply placed on the planet for us to find, step by step, like some elaborate treasure hunt, allowing us, as we increase in intelligence, to gradually discover one apparent fact after another? Some of those with religious beliefs seem to think so, even though the Old Testament story is told in such a way that its logic, or rather its lack of logic, tends to discourage credulity. But the story of Noah's Ark could be looked at in another way altogether. Perhaps our Earth was the Ark – a kind of lifeboat, and all the creatures with us today, including ourselves, rescued from some distant planets threatened by a galactic upheaval – that could be one explanation for the incredible variety of life on our planet. Wild thinking maybe, but if our minds are kept open to every possibility, no matter how far fetched, the more likely we are one day to see at least a glimmer of the truth.

What is the real significance of evolution theory. The broad principles of Darwinism appear to place us as the product of about five hundred million years of a biological selection process, culminating in creatures which, for the first time ever, have acquired the ability to communicate by language. If this is true, why has it taken so long? And is language the last word in means of communication. Perhaps more sophisticated methods of exchanging information once existed, or still exist if only we knew how to use them. Are we still evolving? Not much sign of it in the physical sense nor, it seems, in intelligence. But the recent, on a geological time-scale, explosion of knowledge and the availability of it to a much greater populace than ever before, may have led us to assume some sort of evolutionary progress. Why have we and all the other creatures on the planet evolved in different ways? Does the genetic similarity between us and many other animals mean that we have necessarily had a common origin? The genetic difference between us and them does not anyway seem to be enough to explain our overall variation. Is there for example any evidence that our nearest 'relative' the chimpanzee, is evolving to achieve human capabilities, or even has any need to 'progress' in that direction?

When we tried, in earlier chapters, to identify the true nature of consciousness, we had hoped that there would be a single scientific, or philosophic, view of the phenomena. Apart though from a general consensus that the conscious self relies on the brain for its ability to communicate, the subject is still wide open for debate. When we think without communicating, perhaps trying to solve a difficult problem, in the dark with no external input, and even giving ourselves a headache, could the elusive 'self' which is using the thinking process, be nonetheless operating in another dimension altogether? But when we sleep it also seems, partly at least, to be at rest. And under modern general anaesthetic it appears to have switched off altogether. Not much sign there of 'self' being independent of brain or body. Yet somehow that 'self' returns to life with all its memories intact. So perhaps, as I said in chapter two, about gradually losing the precious gift of self awareness and personality in old age, all may not be lost, anymore than when we are anaesthetised. Could our total memory and personality still exist in some quite independent medium even though our physical brain can no longer access it? These thoughts may seem too unscientific to be taken seriously, and easily contradicted by current well established brain theory, but are they any more implausible than all the other inexplicable physical phenomena that govern our daily lives?

What is the real nature of gravitation, or the transmission of light? Why do electrons continue (for ever?) to rotate about their nucleus? What keeps planets rotating about their parent stars? What is their source of energy? Einstein's relativity theories, and later contributions to the subject, which many of us find difficult to comprehend, have been an incredible advance in understanding the rules which appear to govern these electromagnetic phenomena, but much of their physical structure remains as elusive as ever.

The composition of matter, which we would like to think of as just combinations of molecules made up of atoms, now seems to have been exposed as including a multitude of different particles and forces all apparently interacting with each other. Who invited them all to the party? Are they all essential to the stability of matter, or has Nature reluctantly had to find a home for them?

We know a lot about gravity. We know what it does and we have devised a host of rules which accurately predict its behaviour. We use it with confidence to weigh microscopic items or to control the re-entry of spacecraft or to land on the moon. But we do not know what it is or how it works. This most fundamental everyday component of our environment which affects almost everything we do is still a mystery. When I let go of a stone which I have been holding a few feet above the ground, some kind of attractive force apparently emanating from the ground beneath it (or could it be a propulsive force coming from the space above it) tells it to move directly downwards. That force cannot be observed yet it holds our planet in its orbit round the sun. It holds the whole universe together. Some scientists report the detection of 'gravitational waves', faint signals from outer space, but are never able to describe with any conviction how this invisible force actually operates. Could there instead be some process whereby electromagnetic pressure waves operate throughout the universe, in all directions, causing solid matter to coalesce by the screening affect of its bulk? At least that would avoid having to contemplate an attractive or negative force. Whatever the theory, action at a distance, without any apparent communicating medium, remains one of the greatest unsolved mysteries of nature.

Magnetic forces are similar in some ways but we cannot see them. Magnets can be made to repel each other as well as attract, and I can pass my hand between them without feeling any sensation. Static electricity is another mystery. Just watch grains of rice jumping about inside a transparent plastic container. One day we may develop the long sought unified field theory which will link all these static, electrical, magnetic and gravitational forces, but even then will we know their actual mechanism?

The transmission of light, itself only one small part of the electromagnetic spectrum, seems to defy all reason. Whether we try to cope with Newton's earlier preferred theory that light travels as a stream of particles, or with Maxwell's later concept that it behaves like waves in an electromagnetic field, or with Einstein's reasoning that, in certain circumstances light behaves as packets of quantized energy which we now call photons, none of those great thinkers ever expressed certainty in the matter. Current concepts seem to indicate that all three theories have their place in the total picture of the behaviour of light. But we are still left with a seemingly impossible contention. Are we supposed to be satisfied when we are told by some scientists that the mystery of the transmission of light has now been unambiguously resolved?

To begin with we have to accept that every particle or wave of daylight that reaches our eyes has been, only eight minutes before, some 90 million miles away in a seething nuclear conflagration we call the sun.

But what happens to those packets of information when they arrive? In the example which I most often like to quote I suggest that we consider an ordinary sized illuminated room and imagine a small point about the size of a pinhead in mid air in the middle of the room. Now through that point, at any one moment, there passes a packet of information (perhaps the word 'particle' would be more appropriate) a particle of reflected light from every molecule of solid matter in the room that is not hidden by some intervening object. These particles convey precise details of brightness, texture and colour, and instantly respond to changes and movement. If we try to guess just how many molecules of matter in the room are, in one second, sending out particles of light, all passing through that one point in the room, a trillion would be a serious underestimate. Yet those particles all seem to manage the journey without interfering with or corrupting the directional or spectral integrity of each other. Add to that the fact that on their way they also have to pass through millions of other similarly congested points in the room and the whole thing becomes just impossible. And they all then arrive at other objects in the room, only to be modified again by those objects' colour, texture, etc. and then re-emitted to join the fray again. We are told that different materials absorb different parts of the spectrum of incoming light, and that what we see as the colour of a substance is the re-emitted unabsorbed portion of that light. Black of course is invisible – the text on this page is invisible – since it absorbs all the frequencies of light. What we see in this case is the full spectrum of light coming from the white paper that surrounds each letter or digit.

But what is the actual process when light falls on a molecule that enables it to respond continuously in that way? Each molecule, with its component atoms and their electrons, seems to have the ability to constantly and simultaneously handle millions of incoming light waves, or particles, travelling at 300,000 km (186,000 miles) per second, from a wide visual field. Apparently that molecule, together with its companions, can then instantly analyse those multiple frequencies, absorb some which may then be partly re-emitted as heat energy, and re-emit the unabsorbed frequencies, which we see as its colour, again as spherical waves of light particles, again at 300,000 km per second, also over a wide visual field. They must be very clever, very fast, and very busy, molecular machines !

How can all this happen without mutual interference between light waves or particles in transit? The scientific explanation appears to say that the speed of light, and the way in which waves of light maintain their directional integrity, ensures adequate space for each individual signal to transit without corruption from billions of similar emissions from all the other molecules, both adjacent to it and over the total field of visible matter in the same area. But the often expressed analogy with waves of water crossing each other while maintaining some of their integrity does not seem to be a valid comparison since, in that case, we have two identifiable supporting mediums – water and air, whereas with light no known medium exists apart from an assumption that it forms part of the electromagnetic spectrum. If we ever discover such a medium there is a name already waiting for it – the 'ether' – bequeathed to us from many past centuries of searching.

And we can ask many more questions. Do we have to accept that light re-emitted from an object is passing the incoming light at twice the speed of light? Does a mirror's reflected light pass the incoming light at twice 300,000 km per second? If I shine a concentrated light source, perhaps even a laser beam, at its reflection in a mirror the reflected beam must encounter the light coming from it. Surely it must frequently occur that incoming and outgoing waves or particles meet head on, and collide at twice the speed of light. Will the latest massive CERN particle accelerator near Geneva be able to discover what happens, and why?

And as if that were not enough we have to try our credulity yet further by including, in that already congested small point in space, many other passing pieces of information. There is a component of every one of hundreds of radio and television signals, plus the Earth's magnetic field and that elusive force of gravity, plus a few thousand neutrinos, all this taking place in our room's highly mobile atmosphere which already includes air molecules, sound waves, dust particles and heat radiation. How can we possibly accept such a preposterous contention? Can we think of a better one?

Suppose we go outside into the daylight. On a recent wander in the open country I sat for a while on the top of a hillside and looked across a beautiful valley. On the other side I could see trees and shrubs and open grass. Now my current knowledge told me that every leaf, every blade of grass, every branch and rocky outcrop, that were receiving sunlight, were modifying that light to reflect their colours, textures etc., and then re-transmitting that light (still at 300,000 km per second of course) in all directions, such that any observer in line of sight could see, as I did, a complete picture of the valley. In other words every microscopic spec of space in line of sight of that scene contained at any one moment all the information needed for me, or anyone else, to get a complete picture of that view. And remember, as before, all those streaming packets of retransmitted light had to cross each others' paths, and the paths of the incoming sunlight, billions of times, apparently without any corruption of their messages. Consider the process of taking a digital photograph of that scene. In a tiny fraction of a second my camera could receive and record about five million of those packets of light, each with its precise detail of colour, textures etc. And a thousand other cameras nearby could, in that same instant, record almost identical detail. How can all that information maintain its integrity through such dense multi-directional electromagnetic traffic?

Another example I like to dwell on looks at the other extreme. Consider a star say a couple of million light years away in space. The galaxy Andromeda will do – just about visible to the naked eye on a clear night. We are told that it radiates in many parts of the electromagnetic spectrum and that visible light is a very intense component of it. Imagine one small particle (for want of a better word) of that light. It starts its journey from the star amongst a dense mass of similar companions, all travelling at 300,000 km per second. As the years pass its companions get less and less evident but the one we have adopted continues on its way for hundreds of thousands of years, never slowing, never changing its direction, except perhaps when it passes too close to some other star's gravitational field, until it finally approaches our planet.

One dark night I am looking up at the stars and our small particle of light, still at 300,000 km per second, lands in my eye. After two million lonely years it suddenly ceases to exist, as my brain converts it into an electrical signal that tells me, along with signals from other particles following close behind it, that I have just seen a star. There is no grand celebration to mark the completion of that incredible two million year journey. No recognition of a job well done. It is all too commonplace. And of course not all of its companions complete the journey. Many are absorbed by our atmosphere.

But what keeps it going on its long journey, and why so precisely and consistently 300,000 km per second? And surely that remote star must fill the whole universe, or at least two million light years in all directions, with identical particles of its light. What density of particles must have to commence that journey from Andromeda to provide sufficient density at the entire circumference of a sphere of two million light years' radius, so that each of us, wherever we are, can receive a steady image? And remember there are billions of other stars doing likewise.

So if we are astounded by the magnitude of the density of activity – information in transit – in our small room, or in a valley in the countryside, have we any chance at all of even beginning to comprehend the same process in the whole universe? And of course we must also always keep in mind that what we see may no longer exist or even still be in the same place. All we appear to know in the case of Andromeda is that it was there two million years ago.

It seems that, in spite of many claims to the contrary, the nature of light has still not been unambiguously identified. Whether we think of it as particles or photons or waves of energy, this elusive component of the electromagnetic spectrum, while it conforms to a set of physical laws, does its business without betraying its physical structure. And what about all the other frequencies – the radio waves, the infrared, the ultraviolet, the X-rays, the gamma and cosmic rays. Unlike the visible light rays, the others are normally invisible and we need special apparatus to detect their presence. Many frequencies, including radio, also seem to be able to pass through all but the densest matter without significant corruption. Also, in spite of the incredible volume of electromagnetic activity about us all, a radio message can still find my mobile phone wherever I happen to be in the UK, and also to a great extent on the planet. Scientists simply draw our attention to the unique frequency allocated to each transmission and matching receiver, but is that supposed to be enough to suppress our incredulity?

So if electromagnetic science can provide only the laws that govern nature's physical systems, rather than their actual physical structures and motivations, could electrochemical, or biochemical, processes that function in almost all life forms be a more rewarding field of enquiry. Perhaps that could at least give us a clue to consciousness? Here again though, in spite of almost daily advances in our understanding of the structure of the brain and such successes as the unravelling of the DNA molecule in the human genome project, the search for the location of that elusive 'self' continues to elude us. Also, as observers of the world about us, we cannot fully comprehend how what we experience reaches our brains in the first place, let alone how we process all that detail, and do it with such efficiency. And the DNA discoveries themselves, while explaining how the various components interact, again seem unable to tell us what drives them to do so. What motivates all the life processes, even the sperm to invade the egg?

Nature is remarkably obedient to its laws and we make good use of them all, and scientists have given us many complex formulae for the behaviour of materials and natural phenomena but, as with light, they seem to leave us with little help when we try to envisage how those laws actually apply in practical terms. What do they all mean to the incredulous human mind?

And we might do well to ask how such a complex system could evolve in the first place without the oversight of a superior intelligence. How does theology deal with the problem?

7. A THEOLOGICAL VIEW

The origins of religious belief

The present preoccupation of some of us with this mysterious life force which we all possess, is of course nothing new. Over thousands of years our ancestors, or at least those who had time to spare from their daily efforts to stay alive, have been troubled by such questions. Perhaps, in the absence of ready practical answers, and rather than leaving the matter unresolved, they turned to the idea of some kind of invisible entity or deity to whom they could look for comfort. Whether they consciously created their gods, or whether some revelation actually happened, the then inexplicable and sometimes frightening forces of nature would probably have compelled them anyway to assume god-like causes. Whatever their origins, we have today a world of many religions.

We are each the sum total of our experience from birth onwards, including those characteristics we are born with which affect the way we interpret that experience. So we each have a different view of the world and have very little control over our acquired knowledge, as that control is itself dependent on our previous understanding, and so on back to our birth. Some will protest that they are capable of 'having an open mind' and I do not object to that – I like to think I am similarly blessed, but the degree of open-mindedness we actually have is very debatable. Even an enquiring mind is dependent on available knowledge, and early indoctrination about a particular religious view may be hard to shake off.

To consider the existence of God in open debate has not always been possible and even now in some parts of the world it still risks imprisonment or even death if their dominant concept is challenged. But we must not forget that it is only a few hundred years since similar intolerance existed in European countries, with remnants of it still affecting lives in such places as Northern Ireland. And new conflicts may even yet be generated by irrational mob incitement in currently evolving Christian / Muslim communities.

In presenting my own views on this I am intensely aware that to many millions of people God is their only comfort. Many in this world exist in terrible conditions or suffer appalling tragedy. God, or at least the conviction that some greater benevolent intelligence is in control, is the far-away light which gives them the courage to keep going, although for some peoples strict adherence to their particular religion could be seen as the root cause of their suffering. Even to those more fortunate in physical terms there is often an emptiness, a lack of a sense of purpose in life. To these also God is necessary. Some have a faith so strong that they can tolerate any amount of debate without fear of losing it. They are indeed fortunate. Others have such a fragile hold on their faith that they dare not listen to any discussion for fear of losing what little they possess.

My own view, at present, is agnostic rather than atheistic. I cannot accept the existence of a God in any of the forms depicted by the world's major religions. That does not mean that I am denying the possibility that some form of superior being could exist who is having some influence over us, although total benevolence does not seem to have been much in evidence. If such a being exists he, or it, must be either partially evil or lacking the power to intervene in the often horrific events that continue to plague the human race. But I have not abandoned the principle of some sort of symbolic ideal superhuman whom we should all aspire to emulate. Neither can I declare that there is no longer any mystery about our existence. We have simply widened our horizons so that yesterday's primitive fears have been replaced by today's ever expanding incredulity about the very nature of Life and the Universe. In the absence of all the facts I am certainly not prepared to close my mind even to the possibility of some kind of creative entity, but that does not bring me any nearer to understanding it all. Even a creator has to come into existence at some stage. The ultimate truth, if there is one, simply moves one step further away from us each time we advance towards it. At the very least I am convinced that there must be some other forms of intelligence, superior to our own, that have contributed to our creation and evolution, and to some extent to the blessings and evils of our time.

Now the problem with that sort of view is that it could have been acquired with the minimum of thought, and that is all too often the way we tend to judge the expressed views of others. But, even if they have devoted much soul searching before arriving at their present opinions, they need to explain their reasoning if we are to value their judgement. So I am attempting here to provide a rational explanation of my current thinking on the subject. Tomorrow I may think differently, but the Christian explanation, and those of some other religions, do not seem to me to have much in common with scientific logic, even though a blind acceptance of their religious explanations for everything could save us from the never ending search for an equally elusive truth in what we perceive to be an essentially materialist world.

Looking at the subject from an atheistic point of view, the following statements would therefor appear to be logical assumptions :

a) Religious beliefs began to appear when humans became sufficiently intelligent to start to seek explanations for those aspects of their environment that were beyond their comprehension, and instinctively attributed the many frightening phenomena of their world which they could not explain, to the workings of some kind of ethereal and superhuman beings.

b) Many religions originated in an attempt to impose a moral code. It was the need to enforce that code that necessitated all the doctrines that became attached to them. And the arguments about the interpretation of those doctrines, and the way they were sometimes used by individual leaders for patronage and unfair discrimination, and to martial support in times of war, subsequently led to the breakup and fragmentation of their basic beliefs. The current complex multiplicity of creeds and subdivisions also resulted from the constraints imposed on different races by their environment and geographical location, resulting in each having different perceptions of their world.

c) The continuing credibility of religions in much of today's world still depends on the need of some sections of mankind to have something to hold on to for support, no matter how irrational it may be, rather than face up to the appalling reality and mystery of their existence on our tiny isolated planet – a speck of matter in a void of infinity and eternity.

d) The centuries of friction between different creeds has meant that each creed's religion has become their unifying focal point and flag of convenience for sustaining and keeping alive conflicts which would otherwise have long since succumbed to logic and reason. But the damage has been done, and some elements of the opposing creeds continue, largely because of a collective insufficiency of intelligence, to suspect each other's intentions and pursue protectionist and aggressive policies – although economic and criminal interests are also sometimes involved.

e) It would be wrong to overlook the often beneficial, unifying and disciplining effects of religions, or at least of some of them, especially where those beliefs encourage and enable dedicated people to carry out selfless support for others who need their help. It would be equally wrong to ignore the comfort that religious beliefs bring to many who are unable to grapple with a more complex theology. And humans still mostly seem to need to belong to, or to feel allegiance to, a group or team – inherited from our distant past when for security we hunted and lived together. Other disciplines than religion can and do of course sometimes achieve the same ends.

f) Assuming that the human race were ever to evolve in a way that it became inclined to dispense with religious views of their world, it would still be necessary to develop two positive statements or criteria for their ongoing survival. First they must acknowledge the unknown and accept that there may be a greater intelligence operating beyond their comprehension. And secondly accept morality as a universal, but entirely secular, discipline.

g) The preceding statements do not remove the need for an explanation for the phenomena of our existence. Neither can they preclude the possibility, or even probability, that there exists a higher form of intelligence which has contributed to the environment in which we have evolved. Whether that intelligence is, or is not, wholly benevolent, and whether it is receptive to the pleadings of mankind, is another matter.

The credibility of all the foregoing statements depends of course on my own level of intelligence, over which I have no control, and on the readers' level of intelligence, which could cause him or her to think otherwise. But there are only two logical reasons for not believing in the existence of God – one that you are too intelligent, and the other that you are not intelligent enough. And none of the preceding paragraphs can preclude the possibility that other dimensions may exist of our perceived reality. Neither can we exclude from our thoughts that a superior intelligent being might occupy one or more of those dimensions and be capable of affecting our lives. Name that being 'God' if it helps.

So is it possible that we could ever achieve the transition from a partly religious based morality with its implied discipline of divine retribution, to an entirely secular based morality with its only discipline of community justice, which could be perceived as punishing only those whose crimes had been detected?

But we must not lose sight of the fact that regardless of the degree of adherence to the often conflicting beliefs of the main religions, it is perhaps their associated moral codes and ways of life which matter most to the structure and stability of their communities. I have attempted to deal with this aspect in chapter 11.

So how do all the world's religions, and their sub-divisions, inter-relate.

8. RELIGIONS OF THE WORLD

Is there any prospect of consensus?

There are many religions practised on this planet, some with vastly different concepts of the nature of their gods. Most of them have multiple subdivisions, each with their own complex interrelationships, together with historical advocates who are assumed to have had the authority of their gods, or even in some cases are revered as gods themselves.

There is of course a vast amount of literature about all the world's religions and their evolution over many thousands of years, but even a brief encounter with this subject shows an incredible mass of inter-relating faiths and sub-divisions.

In monotheistic terms the Abrahamic religions could be regarded as the largest group, and if we look at its beginning (*using the Christian calendar*), it became a co-ordinated Jewish religion about 1400 BC, and remained as such until the arrival of Jesus and the emergence of Christianity, which rapidly took hold over a wide area of Europe and Mediterranean countries. By then the original Jewish version had become known as Judaism. But by 600AD Muhammad had appeared, converting many to Islam, adding another division to the original creed. Islam also subsequently split into Sunni and Shiite versions as, many centuries later, did Christians into Catholics and Protestants. However, The Old Testament is still important to Judaism and Christianity and to Islam in the Koran.

Sadly though, all these multiple divisions became the

root causes, or at least the 'flags of convenience', for much of the world's conflicts, and this still applies today. *See chapter 15*.

Faced with such a large disparity in the way in which all these groups practise their religions, there can be little common ground on which to question their assumptions. While I am not prepared to challenge most of them, even if I were competent to do so, I feel reasonably entitled to question some of the beliefs of my own inherited Abrahamic religion, which is Christian, and this I have dealt with in chapter 9.

Looking at the following chart, which attempts to show all the main religious divisions, can we ever hope for a coming together, whether it be an atheistic or religious consensus, that will enable the human race to emerge into the daylight of, at the very least, mutual respect. The major religions are shown in order of magnitude, although if we consider those who actually practise their religions the Islamic content probably exceeds that of the Christian. There are hundreds of smaller branches not shown, plus many independent religions of 30 million or less, including Sikhism, Taoism, Judaism (from which Christianity and Islam emerged), Baha'i and Confucianism, all with subdivisions and some historic links with the major groups. All figures are very approximate and were obtained from several sources, each with substantial variations in content.

The chart also refers to atheist, agnostic and deist, and suggests an approximate figure of 500,000,000. In practice of course, without an honest declaration by all the planet's population it is impossible to know how many are pretending to follow one discipline while secretly believing otherwise. The undecided believer could be agnostic, while the deist is generally defined as having a firm belief in one god, but without the need for any of the doctrines and rules associated with religions revelations. (*See Chapter 10*)

WORLD RELIGIONS

Approximate numbers for each of the main religions

Christian:-		
Roman Catholic	1,100,000,000)	
Protestant	675,000,000)	
Orthodox	200,000,000)	total 2,275,000,000
Anglican	100,000,000)	
Others	200,000,000)	

Sunni Islam & Shia Islam	1,300,000,000

Hinduism	1,100,000,000

Buddhist:-		
Mahayana & Theravada		
Buddhism	330,000,000)	
Shinto & Japanese	)	total 620,000,000
Buddhism	180,000,000)	
Chinese Buddhism	110,000,000)	

Tribal	240,000,000
Chinese folk religions	180,000,000

Smaller religions of 30m or less	100,000,000

Professed atheist, agnostic and deist	500,000,000

TOTAL	6,215,000,000
Estimated world population (2006)	6,500,000,000

9. PROBLEMS WITH BELIEF

The fragility of faith

From an agnostic layman's point of view, i.e. without the benefit of the expert's complex theology, the main difficulties with Christian and some other beliefs are:

1. If there existed a God in the form depicted by Christian teaching, with the powers attributed to him, then it is inconceivable that he would allow such appalling suffering to be endured by so many millions of our kind. For far too long we have been told about the gift of 'free will' and listened to the verbal contortions of various church preachers as they try to explain the absence of God's intervention in the latest horrific tragedy.
2. The notion of free will assumes that we are entirely free to use it, which of course we are not. There are so many forces affecting our lives, totally beyond our control as individuals, that to consider God as being somehow restrained from helping us out of fear of removing that 'benefit' seems illogical. At best it leaves God as somewhat less than all-powerful.
3. It is implied that salvation is available only to those who have faith. I have never been happy with this since it appears to condemn all those who, due to accident of birth or other experiences since birth, have not been able to acquire that faith.

4. Christianity is associated with a mass of obligatory beliefs which tend to obscure the fundamental principles for peaceful living which Christ tried to expound. His teaching seems to have taken second place to an endless variety of arguments about his identity and the correct form of worship. The large number of denominations is ample evidence of this, and it is a person's origin, and subsequently acquired knowledge, which conditions him to adopt a particular denomination, or none at all.

So does that leave anything of the Christian view? It certainly leaves Christ, but it also leaves us with his predecessors such as Abraham and Moses and a host of other prophets. And we also have to consider the Islamic prophet Muhammad, who six hundred years later is said to have delivered a more perfect view of God's will than the Christian message.

Sadly, the teachings of both Christ and Muhammad have sometimes been misinterpreted, by a few extreme factions. as condoning violent oppression of all those who have other religious views. Christian and Islamic history is full of violent internal religious conflicts, even though both disciplines preached tolerance. So we are left with the old question of whether, on a human evolutionary time-scale, the recent advent of religions has brought any lasting benefits to mankind.

But most religions initially started by trying to bring some morality and, perhaps even more important, some kind of cosmic identity, to the otherwise lonely and unprotected human race. So if we were to lose that fundamental traditional religious framework, we would have to find some other faith or moral code, that was acceptable to far more of the human race than to those divided by the present confused jumble of beliefs. And this should take account of all the other religions, outside the Christian / Jewish and Islamic folds.

Is there a rational alternative to the present confusion – one which excludes unquestioning belief?

10. RATIONAL ALTERNATIVES

Is there another way to know God?

The sad fact about the almost universal concept of God is that over the centuries it has presented us with a picture of some sort of super-human being residing in a heaven which defies current physical definition. Those who find this ethereal concept unacceptable due to its physical incompatibility consequently discard the whole notion of God and thereby perhaps lose much that could be worth retaining. It seems that current concepts of the nature of God have unintentionally contributed to a degree of ultimate unbelief. Many religions contain this inherent mechanism which is sooner or later triggered by their followers' realisation that there appear to be rational scientific explanations for much of the phenomena previously attributed to God. The real problem though, is that God originally had to be presented in a form that was readily understandable to multitudes of people who could not necessarily be expected to accept a more complex theology. And that still largely applies today.

So it could be said that the human race has been 'taken for a ride' by a few who have sold them various tales about their origins and gods. All humanity split up by a multiplicity of beliefs and creeds. And each segment mostly persuaded to think that their particular version of God is the only true one. Except that is for a considerable proportion who have no beliefs at all and who seem to be largely unaware of, or are unconcerned about, the mystery of their presence on this planet.

Perhaps everyone should wake up and face the known facts and not allow themselves to be blinded by totally illogical beliefs. We have to acknowledge that there is an awful mystery about our existence. Some are unaware of it, and some are aware but afraid to think about it at all, preferring the comfort of religious doctrines, no matter how illogical they may be, than to acknowledge the admittedly frightening but more rational, though incomplete, theories based on scientific observation.

And only a few seem to have taken the time to indulge in some rational thinking. To have contemplated the reality of our tiny planet in an infinite universe and in an eternity of time. And to wonder why, in that eternity, and in the few billion years of our planet's existence, and the few hundred thousand years of human existence, that we have come to believe intelligent mankind and the gods of our time have only recently appeared. We need brains at the very least capable of emerging from the confines of contemporary history and grasping the sheer magnitude of our own planet's time scale. Only then will we be able to see ourselves for what we are, a minute spec on the face of geological time.

But could we instead redefine God as some sort of abstract creation, a product of the collective human mind, a mental image of an ideal person which we should all aspire to emulate, and simply accept that His existence as originally portrayed, in many different races, was the only explanation available to them at the time for the frightening manifestations of their physical world. Since current theology does not anyway demand a physical presence, the God in this abstract form could equally be said to exist. The laws currently attributed to God have essentially evolved from the natural laws necessary for collective survival, and our much better understanding of the physical world could remove the need for a more mysterious being.

Once we have redefined God in this more abstract form it might open the way for the mass of non-believers to come back into the fold. They would no longer be excluded by unacceptable physical contradictions. God instead becomes the ideal, albeit very difficult to achieve, and to which we should pray, having installed him, so to speak, in our consciences. Or is that where He has really resided all along, a power for good which we all unconsciously possess but all too often ignore. But would this realisation result in better or worse moral standards than those achieved by the present, but less than universal, fear of a more ethereal God?

We cannot of course ignore the concepts of atheism, agnosticism, paganism and pantheism. The atheistic view excludes God entirely, while the agnostic leaves the matter open to debate. Paganism, or at least its contemporary expression, demands allegiance from no one, but tries to extricate us from what it regards as the distortions and dogmatism of Christian and other religions. It is essentially un-dogmatic and its modern manifestation attempts to address contemporary moral concerns, but still has a kind of religious or pantheistic (divine reality) association.

Somewhere in this direction lies Deism, the basic concept of one universal supreme being, with no need for any of the multiplicity of diverse religious creeds which seem to lie at the root of much world conflict.

Over two hundred years ago in 1794 Thomas Paine, whose rationalist ideas contributed much to the American revolution, and subsequently the French revolution, wrote 'The Age of Reason', in which he brought that same rationalism to bear on the world's religions.

He saw in Deism the essence of God as representing all that was beyond our understanding. He made no attempt to envisage that being in some kind of superhuman form or to see any need for human representatives of God such as Christ or Mohammed, although he did not deny their praiseworthy moral attributes.

But his almost impeccable logic seemed unwilling to explain the suffering of the innocent. He saw God as good to all mankind and did not question His failure to prevent that suffering. Also his contention that tyranny in religion was 'the worst of all the tyrannies that afflicted mankind' did not appear to acknowledge the inevitability of its evolution. The higher intellects of ancient history could be content with a simple concept of one, hopefully benevolent god. But in the early more isolated communities of our world their less intelligent populace, probably the majority, could not grasp such a concept without some kind of tangible framework, a moral creed perhaps, and God needed to be envisaged in a human form. So each national leader, working without any knowledge of the existence of each others' communities, formed their own particular creeds, resulting in all the conflicting religions of today.

The damage was done, albeit largely with the best motives, as each leader did his best to bring his community to respect their own versions of a moral code.

But could we extract from all the main religions, including Deism, plus their atheistic counterparts, some fundamental wholly secular morality. A universally acceptable code of conduct which could unite us all without denying each creed their individual religious persuasions?

11. SECULAR MORALITY

Across an uncharted sea without a pilot

In the last hundred years or so there have been many voices proclaiming that evil deeds committed in the name of God have far exceeded those carried out by non-believers. Those who hold such views certainly have considerable evidence to support them but they do not, apart from the communist governments, have much experience of a major country officially excluding religious based morality, and even there the religious component often remained as a hidden influence in many areas of daily life.

Many people are also unwilling to accept a secular view of their evolution and contemporary existence because it requires them to cope with a concept that is at the very least too complex to understand and ultimately too incredible and frightening to contemplate. Religious views are preferred, in spite of their contradictions, and in spite of the need to accept suffering as something God is apparently unable or unwilling to prevent.

Secularism seems to have been largely the product of the more affluent parts of the world, providing we ignore the recent, in historical terms, imposed secularism of the communist countries. As soon as any country achieves a certain degree of prosperity the ability to impose morality by the threat of divine retribution diminishes, since many of those who have achieved wealth become less susceptible to religious exhortations. Morality simply becomes incorporated into legal systems as well as being freely adopted by those individuals, of religious or secular persuasion, who regard it as a duty imposed by their own consciences.

Communism on the other hand, and its dominant creed of Marxism, arose in Europe in the first place mainly as a revolt against the inherited or acquired privileges of royalty and major industrial employers. Although much of the theory was initially developed by Karl Marx and Friedrich Engels in Germany and England, it took hold initially in eastern European countries especially in Russia. But in Russia it was largely the privileged classes' double standards, in which they used their religion as a kind of bastion of conservative elitism, that resulted in the Marxist rejection of religion as a basis for moral discipline, although that rejection was part of a greater effort to dispense with all the trappings of what was regarded as outdated thinking processes.

Marxism itself became a kind of secular religion, and its moral ethics differed little in principle from Christian teaching, but in the process Russian and latterly other communist governments suppressed much of the entrepreneurial activity which had previously been motivated by substantial profits. They had in effect 'killed the goose that laid the golden egg'. So those countries' subsequent historic lack of commercial success probably owed more to a resulting economy that was not competitive with the rest of the world. But looking at it in another way, it could be said that the rest of the world, meaning the world's industrial giants, simply dominated the world economy by remaining free to immorally exploit their populations.

The foregoing is of course an extremely simplified version of the communist story, and its manifestation in other countries such as China and Cuba has many other complex factors. Sadly though, in most of the countries that tried the Marxist experiment, what was intended to be a more honest and principled discipline, ultimately needed a large degree of dictatorial suppression and imprisonment of free thinking individuals in order to succeed.

However I have not found much evidence of whole communities, even nations with officially secular governments, managing to sustain moral disciplines for long without some acknowledgement of their populations' underlying religious principles, with a well entrenched legal system based on such principles. There can surely be little doubt for example, that the billion or so adherents of Islam on this planet have, in spite of their diverse and often conflicting factions, gained much more stability and unity from the teachings of Muhammad than they have lost from internal conflicts fought in his name. Even the apparently endless dispute between the Sunni and Shi'ite divisions of Islam is only kept alive by extreme factions.

Of course there is always the risk in any such disciplined nation that unprincipled leaders might misuse their religious authority to drag their peoples into war. There are plenty of examples in world history. But without their religious disciplines many of these countries would inevitably have dissolved into even greater multiple conflicts and become even more of a threat to world peace.

It would of course be wrong to suggest that moral principles have arisen only in God-fearing or better-off communities. And Christ himself is quoted as having referred, on several occasions, to poor people having sacrificed their own interests to help others, and certainly did not imply that fear of God was their only motive. But there does not seem to be much hope at present of a purely secular morality becoming a driving force for peace in world human affairs. Most of us are still too strongly influenced by deeply entrenched instincts for self-preservation, inherited from our primitive past. The increase in lawlessness in many countries over the past half century or so has many causes and it is not easy to apportion blame, but a decline in moral values is at least part of the reason. And it is hard to see how international agreements can be enforced within participating countries without each having a very strong internal discipline, and that discipline in a large part of the world's population still means a fear of God.

If a secular based morality is ever to take hold on our tormented planet it will require two fundamental changes in human nature. One is for a universal recognition of the moral common ground that is at the root of all the main religions and the other, far more difficult to achieve, is to instil that morality in the entire human race.

There have been several attempts to advocate secular alternatives to religion which nonetheless have tried to embrace many of those religions' moral ethics. In 1938 an American of Lutheran origins – Frank Buchman, who had previously been promoting a kind of secular morality, formed the Moral Re-Armament Organisation, which proposed the adoption of four basic attributes – namely Honesty, Purity, Unselfishness and Love. Although his ideas gained much support at the time, especially in the years immediately after the Second World War, they ultimately faded from public view.

But the moral concepts of honesty and unselfishness are surely the attributes that should dominate all our attitudes to daily life. They appear in most religions but are largely overwhelmed by, or are associated with, a vast mass of doctrinal beliefs. Except, as I said in chapter 10, the largely undogmatic Paganism where, although the conventional association is with the heathen, the more modern concept pays homage to a kind of divine reality. In other words it acknowledges the natural world and all in it that is beyond our understanding, and above all embraces all moral values. Perhaps more secular than religious.

But even if this morality were to totally emerge from the confines of religion, most of us have, programmed into our brains, a competitive instinct that cannot always be held back by moral restraints.

And whatever arguments we make in proposing secularism as an alternative to religious beliefs, we still have to admit that we are no nearer to understanding our presence on this earth. The proponents of secularism can surely never be content with explaining observable physical phenomena as adequate justification for their cause, so secularism could turn out to be just as fragile a concept as its religious predecessors. Could there also be a danger in demolishing the concepts of religion without providing a rational and total alternative explanation for our existence? It is true that some proponents, such as Pagans, contrive to occupy a kind of middle ground which does not totally exclude the possible existence of a superior intelligence, so for the time being it might be better to emphasise that uncertainty and reassure those who feel that their religious beliefs are being undermined.

But if we did manage to convince humans everywhere that there was no god, what would we have left? Our planet could be likened to a huge ocean liner sailing endlessly across an infinite uncharted sea, with all its passengers having no idea of their destination. A few of those passengers might start to wonder about the unknown hazards that might lay ahead. Suppose one of them went up on to the bridge and reported back to his fellow passengers that there was no one at the helm.

Yet if we accept an entirely secular view, that is what we are faced with. Our planet, hurtling through space (about 100,000 kilometres an hour on its journey round the sun) with no one in charge. No one to care for its 6.5 billion human passengers and countless billions of other creatures !

And much of mankind, perhaps understandably, is afraid to face up to that possibility, of a world without a god figure. Someone to whom they could ask for help when needed. So has that fear itself created today's concept of God? Or more need to care for each other perhaps !

But whatever the truth of the matter, with or without a god, if we try to look at the whole of mankind and ignore the multiplicity of reasons both religious and political which set so many creeds and races against each other, there remains the underlying far more immediate and profound challenge which confronts us all, and that is the need to face up to the reality of our situation on this tiny planet. If we think of the Earth as our only lifeboat we might be less inclined to endanger it. If it sinks we have nowhere else to go. If this fundamental human predicament could be placed at the top of the international agenda, and all world's problems were considered with that constantly in mind, we might have less conflict.

Time perhaps to cast aside for a while all our contemporary inherited baggage of beliefs and assumptions and try to take an entirely uncommitted view of the human state.

12. THE HUMAN PREDICAMENT

Looking for a guiding light

We need to define the human situation in a way that clearly expresses our essential needs if we are to live in some kind of harmony, both amongst ourselves and with all the other creatures that together contribute to the environment of this planet. Our predicament must be described in a form that embraces the human race as a whole and that means everyone from the depths of poverty and starvation to the heights of affluence. Whether those needs also include some kind of cosmic identity or faith will, I hope, emerge from these thoughts.

The foundation of our predicament is of course this planet which some of us call Earth, upon which we all find ourselves. In another comparison, it is as if we have all woken up to find ourselves on a train, with no recollection of where it came from and no idea where it is going, with many of the passengers, for that is all we are, seeming content to accept the narrow view of their train compartment, and not even bothering to look out of the window. These represent perhaps the majority of the human race, who are too preoccupied with their daily lives even to be aware of their place in the cosmos. They are perhaps in many ways fortunate for they are not troubled by infinity or eternity, nor by the preposterous fact of their very existence. Even those who do dwell occasionally on the matter see no need to look beyond the comfortable theory of evolution, which to them is the whole truth rather than just part of it. They do not suspect the work of a superior intelligence in the design of their own minds and bodies, in the miracle of birth or the incredible complexity of the physical universe.

Yet those of us who do attempt to dwell in depth on the full significance of what we assume to be reality, and who do so without the comfort of a conventional religious explanation, have to face up to the appalling precariousness of our lonely abode in the cosmos. Here we are, along with more than six billion other humans and countless other creatures, travelling through space on a tiny revolving planet, closely circling a star, a huge ball of burning matter into which some slight perturbation could surely send us plunging at any moment. The totality of this truth, and any additional truth about the nature of a superior intelligence, if it were revealed to us, would be more than most of us could cope with. But what do we mean by reality? And what is this 'real world' that we keep trying to define?

There are two fundamental factors which stand in the way of truly understanding our cosmic identity. For those of us who think about it, how can we accept the apparent infinity of space and the apparent eternity of time? What for instance exists beyond the perceived universe? Is nothing just empty space? And time has no finite measure other than our own perception of it. A minute to a man might seem like an hour to an ant. The scientists' concepts of space time can only present us with sets of equations which, even for those few who can understand and marvel at their mathematics, do little to enable us to envisage their practical significance.

So any attempt to give the human race a location in both time and space has to acknowledge those limitations from the start. Our usual day to day framework for living might recognise our immediate ancestor's times and perhaps think a few years ahead when we plan our own futures. We might occasionally think about the last two or three thousand years or even contemplate aboriginal tribes say twenty thousand years ago. But we know with some certainty that creatures like ourselves lived over two million years ago and that trees very similar to today's trees existed five hundred million years ago. And the Earth we are told could have been formed nearly five thousand million years ago.

And where does that leave us, the human race? Seemingly no more than a brief incident in the aeons of eternity, and a very lonely fragment of life in the apparent infinity of space.

So having acknowledged ourselves to be no more than apparently minor players in the history of our planet, is there any evolutionary contribution at all to which we can credit , or debit, our brief existence?

The Earth could have, and probably has, hosted more civilizations than those for which we have found evidence. Fossilized remains indicate various life forms existed hundreds of millions of years ago but can we be sure about their degree of intelligence? It is all too easy to judge them in current human terms. Some life forms may not have needed the technological trappings we regard as essential. Consequently they would not have left behind the kinds of objects and structures we tend to regard as evidence of intelligence.

It all seems too improbable that we are the first creatures on this planet in about five hundred million years able to modify, intentionally or otherwise, their environment. Have all the previous ice ages and other global upheavals had entirely natural causes rather than being the result of the then current life form's destructive activities? If we are the first then we have to ask why. What, after all that time, happened to produce a life form that was so different from all that had gone before? Did some random modification in Nature's universal DNA structure suddenly release us into the environment?

There are many structures and artefacts which, if the human race were to become extinct, would remain as evidence of our time on Earth. But for how long? Assuming no major geological upheaval our modifications to the landscape, in the form of say major canals and tunnels, might probably last longer than anything else. But would they still be in evidence a million year's later? Concrete would not, and the pyramids of Egypt will probably only last several thousands of years especially as much of their outer stone cladding has been plundered.

Consider the various metal structures and objects? Bridges of course would be gone in a few hundred years, but objects made of more refined metals like stainless steel could last much longer, assuming they were preserved in a place free of certain other metals, chemicals and extreme temperatures.

But we are still thinking at most in millions of years. Surely civilizations, comparable to or even less primitive than ourselves, could have existed hundreds of millions of years ago with no trace remaining long enough for us to find today. We place much credence on fossils but there are still many gaps left to fill in our planet's paleontological history.

However, all this conjecture does not alter our present predicament. Somehow we have to face up to reality as we currently perceive it, though even then will we ever be truly able to see and fully understand ourselves?

So where do we start in any attempt to find a way out of this awful mess that the human race has got itself into? There is cosmic identity or faith, there is morality, and there is the desperate need to realise the limited capacity of our planet to sustain us all.

It is no good expecting the starving millions to spend time reconsidering their faith. It is equally unlikely that a man with a starving wife and children will stop stealing food, if that is the only way left to him, simply because we tell him it is immoral to do so. And the limited capacity of his part of the planet to sustain his community seems to have no effect on his escalating birth rate. From our comparatively comfortable standpoint it is not easy to see the harsh reality that dominates his view of the world, but it is evident that we must look elsewhere for a starting point.

What about the comparatively well-off part of humanity? Can they produce some acceptable discipline or ideology that would benefit all mankind? The affluent would never agree to reduce their standard of living to a level which gave all the world's population an equal share of food and energy resources. So this disparity appears to be an unresolvable and permanent source of conflict. But they might respond, as perhaps they already are doing to some extent, if they realised that their world was threatened by the ever growing third-world population. There is some concern but it does little more than cope with current disasters and provide the occasional financial or economic concession.

But two contradictory factors have to be acknowledged. One is that the high birth rate in some of the poorest countries is balanced by a high death rate due to starvation and disease. Surely the more we help them to survive the greater is the ultimate problem. One child saved today could mean ten to be saved a generation later. So we have an apparent vested interest in letting their death rate increase. Not that our compassion would ever allow it. And the other factor is that if we do not help them then they become compelled more and more to over exploit and lay bare their parts of the planet just to stay alive. And that is bad for us all.

What we seem to lack is the one most vital ingredient, a clear direction and destination, a guiding light, a viable future pinnacle to reach for. Could that be the missing key to the survival of us all?

Perhaps we need to look at the economic factors which affect us and the pollution consequences of our presence on this planet.

13. ECONOMICS OF HUMAN SURVIVAL

The real cost of living!

Whether we think about it or not, the lives of most of us are influenced, for better or worse, by world economic decisions. There are many economic factors affecting our complex civilisation and there is considerable imbalance in the way in which individual nations are affected by global fluctuations in monetary values. Much depends on a nation's geography, mineral assets, and governmental stability. Also the success of its products depends on the degree of competition from other nations who might unfairly subsidise their industries. If we look at the available planetary resources, and then relate them to the way we make use of them, it seems impossible that we will ever be able to effect their just distribution.

Assuming a continuing benign environment, the following appear to be the prime sources of support for human survival:

a) Food – requires land – reusable – plus human and fuel energy.
b) Raw materials – partly reusable – require energy to obtain.
c) Energy – requires fuel – mostly non-replaceable.

If we had one unified world, with one world currency and wage rate, and no opportunity for international exchange rate manipulation, then perhaps we might achieve some sort of stability. The availability of the above resources would then affect us all equally, even though the possible consequential restraints on our competitive instincts might inhibit innovation.

The reality is of course much more complicated. Repeated fluctuations in supply and demand, in employment costs and in some countries' climatic restraints, plus the influence of multiple international interactions, means that continuous monitoring and consequential adjustments are needed in order to maintain some sort of balance in individual countries' economies. There seems to be no way, once a country has participated in international trade, by which its economy can avoid endless challenges to its long term stability. And opportunities exist for massive exploitation of the many to benefit the few.

But another factor is becoming increasingly evident and is forcing us to rethink all our calculations. And that is the entirely negative consequence of pollution and the over exploitation of our planet's resources. There is growing evidence that the current direction of human development is unsustainable. The materials that we burn to fuel what we regard as our basic needs all produce polluting by-products, and sooner or later will be exhausted. Also what is so often forgotten is that by far the most used fuel of all is oxygen – the very thing we all need, in its un-burnt form, to survive at all. And even that supply, most of which is produced by the planet's forests and the oceans' algae, is under threat from deforestation and pollution.

At the time of writing this the most imminent impact of world pollution appears to be global warming, due to the accumulation of combustion byproducts in the upper atmosphere. Already we are witnessing a dramatic melting of polar ice. Sea ice can melt without affecting world sea levels, but ice on land, such as that on Greenland, already melting at an alarming rate will, if it were to melt entirely, cause sea levels to rise by up to five or six metres – enough to flood many of the major cities of the world. Add to that the equally imminent prospect of melting Antarctic ice, also mostly on land, and we are talking of a huge reduction in habitable areas, a world disaster way beyond anything the human race could cope with, Can we do anything now to reduce global warming, or is it already too late? Rather than do nothing we can at least make an effort to curb our excesses.

We need to consider pollution in its entirety – not just the major sources such as the giant power stations, factory chimneys, road and air transport, but also our own personal day to day contribution when we heat or air-condition our homes, use our cars or dispose of our rubbish. About 20 billion tonnes of Carbon Dioxide (CO_2) per year are produced by burning fossil fuels.

But almost all living creatures on this planet also consume oxygen and produce CO_2. Human breathing alone produces nearly 2 billion tonnes per year (*see footnote p85*)

Overall, world pollution has primarily become critical because of over population – note relationship between high density populations in naturally adverse climates, hot or cold, and the consequential need for heating or air conditioning, although two thirds of the so called third world populations can neither afford, nor have access to, such facilities.

Consider nationwide power generation – two hundred years ago it was unheard of. Today we cannot envisage existing without it. In our nonetheless commendable efforts to reduce carbon dioxide pollution we have even embarked on what has turned out to be a dangerous exploitation of the power locked up in the atoms of certain materials such as uranium. Non-polluting in the conventional sense, but having highly hazardous radio active by-products that need to be securely contained for thousands of years.

Consequently there is no immediate prospect of

significantly reducing our dependence on fossil fuels with all their associated unwanted emissions. In a few parts of the world non-polluting hydro-electric power generation is practicable and very successful, but elsewhere we are still in the early stages of developing wind and wave power – possibly even solar energy devices. There are also trials underway using quick growing types of brushwood as a fuel, where the carbon dioxide produced and the oxygen consumed is roughly equal to the oxygen produced and carbon dioxide absorbed in the growing process. But with so much investment in the oil industry there needs to be much more world political will.

We may yet be able to reduce road transport pollution. One highly promising breakthrough seems to be the development of fuel cells, where no actual combustion takes place, electricity being generated by bringing together hydrogen and oxygen through a membrane seeded with platinum. Already some trial vehicles are on the roads in various countries, including some London buses, but there are many technical problems to be overcome before more widespread use is possible, including the difficulty in safely containing hydrogen. A short term compromise might be to use methane which is more easily contained, but each vehicle then needs to carry a hydrogen extraction mechanism. Here again though the oil refiners could hold back development and it could be many years before we are rid of the exhaust fumes and oxygen depletion that threaten the health of us all.

In the end of course, it is ourselves that demand all the energy and materials that the power producers and manufacturers are only too happy to supply. We ask for heating or air conditioning for our homes and work places. We ask for fuel for our cars. We expect our shops to always have in stock food, clothing and furnishings. Most of us have come to regard these things as indispensable. In many senses they are. Our life styles, especially in large towns and cities, have become totally dependent on the complex of interwoven services such as water, gas, electricity, sewage and other waste disposal, food deliveries and transport, that we now need just to survive.

So what can be done? Very little it would appear. We have little hope as individuals of extricating ourselves from such dependence. How can we bring pressure to bear on all the massive industrial giants that dominate our economic structures? In a small way some of us could perhaps cut down on the number of car journeys, or improve our house insulation, or buy locally produced food to help reduce road transport. But how can we stop the crazy process of transporting almost identical foods in both directions across Europe and beyond, just to satisfy those who fancy a change of taste? A truck load of yogurts can produce about a cubic metre of exhaust fumes per pot on a five hundred mile journey. And how can local produce and locally manufactured goods compete when we import much cheaper food and materials from third world countries with low labour charges – achieved in spite of massive transport and pollution costs – often both ways when we send components halfway round the globe to be assembled by cheaper labour and then re-imported? The exploitation of that labour (sometimes even child labour) in overseas poorer countries could even conceal weaknesses in our own economy – we are in effect living beyond our means by not paying the full morally appropriate cost of those products.

Our prime concern must be to preserve our planetary environment. Yet all the UN sponsored efforts so far have produced only a few small steps forward – not by any means enough to stem the rising tide of pollution – only perhaps a slight slowing down as a few countries give it serious attention. Short term economics appear to dominate the issue, plus the seemingly unavoidable difficulties experienced by many poorer countries – the pollution consequences of their industries taking second place as they struggle to compete with the major players. Could our only hope lay in fuel tax increases to reflect pollution costs, and in electric vehicles and non-polluting power generation.

But increased fuel taxes / motorway taxes etc. mostly adversely affect lower income people or small businesses trying to compete with major organisations. The better off car owners for example would hardly notice, so their daily contribution to pollution would not be reduced by increased taxation. Globally enforced taxation of the fuel producers could be another option but international consensus is a very remote possibility and once again we would be penalising poorer countries struggling to compete.

For electric vehicles we have to set the reduced pollution from them against possible increased pollution from central power stations and efficiency losses in transmission, battery charging etc. We must speed up development of fuel cell technology which could reduce transport pollution by at least two thirds. and make more use of wind, tidal and solar power. Massive research and investment is needed in these fields – it could be our only hope.

The situation is becoming increasingly urgent. Do we have to get to the brink of extinction before the dreadful truth sinks in to our collective conscience, and will it then be too late to save ourselves? There is some evidence that we may already be on an unstoppable decline.

What are the prime factors that need to be considered if we and our environment are to survive?

Note: See page 81. Human CO_2 breathed output.

The figure of 2 billion tonnes is based on the assumption that the average human* breathes about 7·5 litres of air **per minute** and the average content is:-

	IN	OUT
Oxygen	21%	16%
CO_2	— —	4%
Nitrogen	78%	79%

So for CO_2 4% of 7·5 litres = 0·3 litres each human per minute.
Human world population is approx 6 billion.
Therefore CO_2 human world emission is 1·8 billion litres per minute.
Weight of 1 litre is 1·98 gms giving us 3,564 tonnes per minute or,
at 525,600 minutes per year = **1·873 billion tonnes per annum.**

* average human – ranges from child to active adult.

14. CRITERIA FOR HUMAN AND PLANETARY SURVIVAL

Is it already too late?

There is only one clear message that has come to us from our unknown origin. Permanently programmed into all mankind, and into all other living creatures and plant life, is the desire to stay alive and to reproduce. Most of us do not question this built-in requirement. Do we ever say "why bother" and simply stop eating. Somehow it is more complex than that. The program also makes sure that any such decision by any living creature would make them very uncomfortable in the process. We are all pre-conditioned in no uncertain manner to keep to the life path by this threat of acute distress if we dare to deviate from it. The difficulties encountered by those who feel compelled to end their lives are a clear example of this.

Can we read a bit more into the message? There is of course the reproductive process. The almost universal procreation device that seems to be intended to ensure that defective genes are progressively eliminated. Does it also ensure progressive improvement? To some extent it does but it may not be able to cope with the challenges of today's ever more demanding environment.

However, there does seem to be a clear indication that nature demands of us some sort of continuing evolution, but in the absence of a purpose can we make use of that fact to guide us in our quest for an adequate survival formula. In the past, primitive evolution depended on the survival of the fittest. The human race has long since confused that process by adding to physical fitness an intelligence factor which sometimes perpetuates the physically unfit. In crude terms we should perhaps not attempt to keep the ill alive, at least while they are still capable of reproducing. If that were the only criterion our quest would be over. Just let the weakest die as nature apparently intended, and that would also mean leaving the starving third world millions to their natural fate. If the fittest help the weak to survive are they not thereby risking the health and future viability of all the human race?

Whatever the cold hard facts appear to dictate, we are not going to be so easily satisfied. Are we sure of those definitions. Should 'fittest' mean just physical fitness? Could third world hardship be a better formula for our ultimate survival than the softer life style of the affluent? What do we mean by intelligence? And what part if any should kindness and compassion play in our thinking? Surely that has evolved for a purpose as well.

The first definition has to include intelligence with physical fitness, not because it makes a clear contribution to survival but because it seems to be the automatic outcome of human evolutionary processes. And the aim of all those enduring hardship is to achieve the 'softer' life style anyway, which could negate any 'benefits' acquired from their experience. As for the definition of intelligence in this context I can only describe it as the ability to be aware of external factors affecting one's present and future situation and to make rational decisions on a course of action. The higher the degree of intelligence the better the decision. Whether the resulting improved capacity to avoid danger is countered by any later detrimental effects in allowing the physically unfit to survive is another question.

Kindness and compassion need a far closer examination. It is all too easy to dismiss these attributes as yet another instinctive contribution to collective survival. Surely if we are kind to others they will be kind to us. We have then ensured that our children will have a more secure world, and help to produce a more caring society for us in our old age etc. But it does not seem to be a built-in attribute, more an accidental acquisition by some of us depending on a combination of intelligence, education and early experience.

And where does the rest of our society fit in, those who have the opposite attitude, the greedy, the careless, the criminals and the criminally negligent? Is that just a lack of intelligence, or do they consciously accept that their actions, or lack of them, will harm their society or even other nations, or make a more hazardous world for their own children? It is almost as if some other evolutionary factor were operating, one which responds perhaps to over-population. In the rest of the animal world shortage of food leads to the survival of the fittest, who in this case are the ones paying the least heed to the welfare of their neighbours. The only exceptions are those caring for their young.

If we have to take account of all these factors how can we hope to see a clear way ahead. I think it is necessary to look at this as a series of priorities. If the primary objective is the continuation of human life then we must protect at all costs the quality of the procreation process and that means a strong emphasis on family obligations and some restraint on population increase. Evolution will follow but since we don't know where it will lead us we can only assume that quality is the key. All the other factors must be subservient to that. But nothing is possible without a conducive environment. How can we save our planet and its environment?

We cannot survive in isolation. The planet and all animal and plant life need to be taken into account. And what happens if we question the contribution that each species makes towards the well-being of our planetary environment. If there were some god contemplating the removal of the most damaging inhabitants then surely the human race would be the first to go. We are the worst thing that ever happened to this planet. In the last hundred years we have used resources that have taken millions of years of creation, and we have produced pollution that will take thousands of years to eliminate. And global warming, as I said in the previous chapter, may already be beyond recovery.

If we really have the planet as our priority perhaps humans should be eliminated. Could intelligence, or at least our degree of it, be an evolutionary mistake, a bizarre mutation which would then disappear and leave the rest of nature to carry on with its old ways? All living things would once again live in harmony with their world. There could be a place for mankind, but only if they were prepared to abide by the rules, like the aborigines in Australia before they were so cruelly disturbed. They did not need 'progress'. They were not going anywhere. They had arrived thousands of years before and found their eternal abode.

Have we got any real advantage over the birds that so freely fly about the skies, or the whales and dolphins who gather their food by swimming joyfully about the seas with their mouths open? In the next few years we will have to come to terms with our planetary environment and learn to live in harmony with it. It is the only way. If we are going to stay here then the survival of all living creatures becomes our responsibility, and our own salvation.

Our first priority is of course population control. In theory our planet could feed twice as many as at present, if food were the only requirement. But energy needs and current world pollution increase seem to indicate that our present population is already far too large. Even if we find ways to substantially reduce CO_2 levels amenable living space is also essential. On all counts a world population of two billion rather than six billion would seem to be necessary for a sustainable environment.

The control of population growth has to be tackled primarily in some of the poorest countries, where poverty is often a direct result of their numbers exceeding their land's capability to sustain them. Governmental mismanagement is also a factor of course, where exploitation tends to go hand in hand with lack of birth control education. It is also tragic that some religious factions continue to object to most forms of birth control, thereby implying that their God is content to see the resulting misery and starvation of most of his followers, who are simply responding to their inherited natural instincts.

But countries cannot simply export their surplus populations to the more prosperous parts of the world. It is not just a matter of the affluent shutting the door on the poor. The wealthier have to some extent achieved their more comfortable state by population limitation. Too great an influx could only bring with it the same increased birth rate and resulting poverty.

That is not the whole picture of course. We cannot ignore history. Much of the so called 'first world' wealth was acquired by exploitation of the 'third world'. Does the former not now have some responsibility for the latter? In some respects it does, but to simply take on surplus populations would only be of temporary help and would probably result in reducing the better managed countries' ability to help. Instead, if for no other reason than their own survival, the wealthier nations must substantially increase their economic support to the poorer countries so that their populations no longer feel the need to seek a better life elsewhere. The wealthier nations owe it to them anyway !

So an essential component of any solution has to be to place all possible emphasis on birth control education throughout the over-populated parts of the Earth and to ensure that their populations clearly associate increased numbers with increased poverty. That we all see overpopulation as leading inevitably to over-exploitation of the planet's resources, with a steady decline in the prospects for survival of the human race and, above all, with the ultimate destruction of our planet's ability to support most other forms of life as well. And population overflow in much of the world also leads to instability and aggression.

But even the more wealthy parts of the world should be looking carefully at their lifestyles. Most of those country's populations, or at least the city dwellers, have become totally dependent on a complex network of services which, if interrupted, could mean a major challenge to their survival. They depend almost entirely for heating, lighting, cooking, water, waste disposal, and remote sources of electricity and gas, and on a nationwide – even to some extent worldwide – food supply chain that needs an equally vast fuel supply to function at all. A failure of electricity in a large city for instance, if it lasted for more than a few hours would, as some of us well know, cause many systems to break down, including not just heating and lighting, but freezer units in homes and supermarkets, sewage pumping systems and water supplies to high rise buildings. Consider the impact of several days or more of loss of such services. Nowhere near enough has been done to anticipate and cope with such a disaster.

Can we have any hope of our human race avoiding the fate that has befallen past civilizations on our planet. Why did they all disintegrate? Certainly conflict appears to have played a significant part, though climatic changes also featured. It could be argued that, unlike the previous examples, we have become a worldwide civilization and therefore more resistant to such collapse. But the multiple hazards we have created for ourselves – nuclear, chemical and biological weapons, any of which could fall into the wrong hands or be accidentally deployed, suggest instead a possible end to all human life, even to all life, without even a residue to restart the process.

However, even if we are successful in reducing our polluting activities and preventing mutual annihilation, there could be an even greater challenge to our future? In chapter five we have already considered how the human body might not be able to survive if all the artificial support that we currently enjoy were suddenly removed. But what if our planet, our only home, ceased for entirely natural reasons to be habitable. Several possibilities, even probabilities, could cause our only life support system in space to become uninhabitable. A major volcanic eruption for instance could result in sufficient atmospheric dust to shut out sunlight for years. Almost all plant life would die and together with the absence of solar heat few land based creatures could survive the starvation and extreme cold. We know it has happened before and the last occasion is thought by some to have occurred about 75 thousand years ago on the island of Sumatra. But further back in time, about 60 million years ago, an even more drastic event appears to have happened. The only insurance against such risk of total annihilation of our race would be to spread ourselves and others of our earth's life forms around several other planets. But since there is not much on offer in our own solar system that would mean travel far beyond anything even remotely within our current capability. All that we could hope for then would be that some of our kind, or at least some other life forms, already exist elsewhere,

At the very least we should learn to have more respect for our home world and try not to waste so much of our time and energy, and our planet's finite life supporting resources, in pointless conflict.

15. CONFLICT AND RELIGIOUS DIVISIONS

A tragic waste of human resources.

In most life forms the principle of survival of the fittest demands repeated tests of that fitness. These tests had to be competitive and originally could only involve some form of aggressive combat.

The human animal has subsequently developed other competitive processes but many of these e.g.. by educational achievement, trading, financial dealing etc., do not have any direct bearing on physical fitness and the consequence of this is often conflict between those who have achieved financial or class superiority and those whose only asset is physical strength.

The instinct for aggressive competition is not a factor which can easily be removed from the human race. It is present in varying degrees in most of us, mainly as a last resort if all else fails, but in some as the only resort. Its use depends on an individual's perception of the degree of threat, real or imagined. Differences become magnified and are sometimes deliberately exploited for personal gain.

There are many other factors which have evolved to enable humans to be competitive without physical aggression, with the result that we are rapidly creating an elite which is substantially physically unfit, or at least incapable of physical competition, relying only on technological superiority to survive, but still finding themselves reluctantly having to use that technology for physical violence as a last resort if they feel threatened.

So there is a prospect of endless conflict between those who rely only on physical aggression and those who rely on non-physical means to sustain their superiority, as each in turn perceives the other to be a threat. The roots of conflict seem to lie in a combination of a collective insufficiency of intelligence, inherited religious differences, overpopulation, un-resolved primal instincts, and greed.

Is there any hope therefore of the human race ever losing its inherent aggressive nature, if by so doing it would lose its basic formula for survival?

Many human brains are not intelligent enough to make reliable rational judgements on complex issues. The majority of humans seem to need clear simple statements on every aspect of their daily encounter with the world they inhabit. Where major issues such as international or racial disputes are concerned they cannot, or do not wish to, enquire into the detailed origins of such problems. They need in effect to find a clear single motive for the conflict and to attribute it to e.g. a single race or class or religion, rather than to particular individuals who happen to belong to, but probably do not represent, their particular race or class or religion.

Conflict usually arises when a particular group of humans feels oppressed or devalued in their community and assume that it is due to their class or race or religion, but often they are simply clinging to any common feature which could unite them. They may in fact be collectively unsuccessful in some way due to accident of birth or history or geography, and not in any way responsible for that state. Others of their community may judge themselves to be superior for similar but equally historic or irrational reasons. Serious conflict is usually generated by only a few of the more extreme elements in a particularly unsuccessful group who then turn to blaming their lack of success on their perceived oppressors, rather than admitting that it might be partially due to their own shortcomings. The problem can then be reinforced by some of the more successful elements in the community who become fearful that their assumed superiority is threatened.

If most of the successful group happen to associate themselves with a particular race or religion that is different from that of their discontented neighbours, that factor becomes the focal point for persecution. A small element in the less successful community, on finding that all normal channels of protest fail to help, then decide to take matters into their own hands and rally support from the majority for aggressive action. In order for that majority to respond, the rallying cry has to be presented to them by depicting the other side's motives in simplified and exaggerated terms.

Strife between those of different religious convictions is rarely what it seems at first glance. It is usually internal rather than international and is often the result of a long history of discrimination in which those in power, both centrally and locally, have unwittingly helped to perpetuate historic divisions by giving preference in employment and other benefits to those of a particular religious persuasion. The dispute is not about religion itself. Similar preferential treatment occurs in some non-religious associations and is still prevalent in many areas of business, government and the civil services, not least in the UK.

This does not imply that the part of the community which perceives itself to be disadvantaged does not have a genuine grievance. That grievance may have remained unresolved for many years and has shown no prospect of democratic resolution. Such situations ultimately breed a few people who can see no other way than to take matters into their own hands.

It is therefore the responsibility of any section of a community which has become significantly more successful than the rest, to take account of the impact of their success on others and to try to contain that success to a reasonable level. They also need to avoid such actions as selective employment and flagrant demonstrations of their assumed success.

Currently there are thirty or more such conflicts ongoing in the World, most of them so protracted that they never make the headlines. In most cases the usual common factors appear, with those more successful in their community unintentionally stimulating discontent among their less successful neighbours, although in the Israeli / Palestinian conflict for example the cause is also rooted in the Palestinians' bitter sense of having much of their country taken from them.

In Northern Ireland a complex situation resulted from the partition of Ireland in 1920, when all but six north-eastern counties achieved independence from the UK. A protracted conflict then arose as certain paramilitary groups, mainly the Irish Republican Army, tried to intervene to defend the interests of a minority Catholic population in the British ruled counties. Their cause was that the predominantly Protestant population was perceived as controlling most of the employment and housing, and discriminating against the Catholic minority. Whether the ensuing terrorist and plainly criminal acts could ever be justified is another matter, but the root cause of the dispute must surely reside in the historic religious intolerance between some elements of the Protestant and Catholic populations, which then gave ample opportunities for a few of more violent disposition to exploit the situation.

The current Islamic internal conflict between Sunni and Shi'ite is yet another sad example of how a community can be split by varied interpretations of their basic creeds. The majority of their populations have no clear understanding of the finer points of dispute and probably have no wish to become involved. But they have become dragged into the conflict by distinctions imposed on them by more extreme factions, again with resulting preferential employment and other discriminations.

In Uganda there was always much conflict between about forty different ethnic groups, and the period of British rule did little to resolve the problem. From early 1900 a gradual influx of Indian labour, originally brought in to work on the new railway lines, resulted in them ultimately taking over much of the commercial business. As so often happens in such a divided community there was much army brutality and when Idi Amin took control he caused economic disaster by expelling almost all of the Indian community. Uganda is still an unstable country although latterly some economic improvements have occurred. But the root cause of all their historic and still ongoing conflicts must again be the intolerance of different racial groups for each other, although corruption and some external economic pressures played a part.

In the 1930's we had the systematic persecution of the Jews, this time in Germany, but not for the first time in their history. Similar treatment had occurred in Russia in the preceding century and is recorded frequently over the past three thousand years. But by far the worst event was the dreadful holocaust of the Jews in the latter half of the 1930's. Why were they so unpopular? Although throughout their recorded history there were many complex reasons for conflict with larger religious groups in their adopted countries, it seems that latterly, for some of them at least, their particular way of life, perhaps their professed exclusiveness, maybe also their commercial and business successes, combined again with preferential employment opportunities, contributed in some degree to their unpopularity and provided fertile ground for Hitler and the Nazis to evolve. A strong factor at least, with their religion becoming their unselective identifying label.

But their troubled history has now led them to a much increased presence in Palestine, which they claim, with some justification, to be their true home. It is not the intention here to comment on the history of this justification, but to question the manner of its interpretation. When the UN, in 1947, authorised the Jews to take over the government of half of Palestine, it led to an appalling increase in confrontation between Jews and Arabs, including conflicts with Lebanon, Syria, Egypt and Jordan. The worst impact was the enforced exodus of Palestinians from much of their land and from their homes and businesses, and Jewish encroachment into those areas intended to be retained solely by Palestinians. Although much of that Jewish encroachment could be considered as justified at the time by the need to defend themselves, it was their subsequent consolidation of those areas with new settlements that resulted in bitter resentment and further so-called 'terrorist' activity. But the history of this conflict is far more complicated than this, with extreme factions on both sides unwilling to compromise, and an incredible multiplicity of past agreements, and broken agreements, affecting the issues. Current dispute (2006) is over the conflicting claims to Jerusalem and the continued reluctance of Jewish leaders to enforce removal of their settlements from all Palestinian West Bank territory i.e.: to withdraw to the 1967 boundaries. This seems to be at the root of much middle-east unrest and its resolution could go a long way towards ultimate peace in the region.

Almost as appalling as the Holocaust of the Jews, was the far more recent genocide in Rwanda in 1994. Here, in spite of earlier interventions by the UN, a long standing conflict between what had been the elite landowning Tutsi tribe and the majority Hutus culminated in the slaughter of over 500,000 Tutsis and the flight of half the 7,000,000 population into neighbouring countries.

Another conflict in central Africa is still ongoing in Sudan. Its roots appear to lie partly in dispute between the largely Christian south, which is rich in mineral resources, and the Muslim dominated north, and also between different Muslim factions. But the activities of some rebel groups and government forces has already claimed the lives of more than 2,000,000 and again has led to millions more refugees in neighbouring countries.

We can find parallels in Bosnia, in Kosova, in Chechnia, in The Congo, in East Timor, in the Solomon Islands and in many other parts of the world. Wherever it happens it is usually rooted in religious differences and or elements of their long term indigenous populations who become fearful, sometimes rightly so, of their traditional way of life being disrupted by the growing population of more recent arrivals, and of finding themselves overtaken by customs, religions and attitudes they could not accept.

In some cases conflict developed because more remote parts of a country's population felt disadvantaged economically. In our own so called United Kingdom we have tried to meet the problem half way and soften the impact. In both Scotland and Wales agitation by vocal minorities to persuade their populace of the need for independence from central government, has resulted in Parliament reluctantly conceding a degree of devolution. Without those concessions we could have seen a more militant expression of discontent, and this may still happen. The real danger in any such situation is that while the original motivation for seeking change is usually a genuine quest for remedying local perceived disadvantage, there is always the risk of exploitation by more militant elements, and the proponents of change should always bear this possibility in mind.

Could we go back much further into history and consider also the prehistoric inbuilt survival instincts which ensured dominance of the strongest species, even at the earliest bacterial stage. This instinct, because of its continued, ever increasing success, became more and more established in the gene structure of all living creatures.

Although limited food resources were a primary factor in stimulating species dominance, the human species has inevitably inherited this by now deeply entrenched instinct, and in spite of thousands of years of evolution we are not yet collectively capable of ignoring its all pervasive presence. But this original instinct has long ago lost its fundamental survival related function and appears instead to latch on to any class or racial characteristic, no matter how minor, and become an excuse for quite unjustifiable and irrational intolerance.

However, the violent consequences of any period of such intolerance, no matter how irrational their original cause, can leave a legacy of bitterness which itself then becomes self perpetuating. So the problem then becomes how to break the cycle. It would be nice to think that all that is required is to explain what has happened to the opposing parties and they would then make peace with each other. But evil is always there, waiting in the wings, ready to intervene and turn any simple conflict of interests into a violent confrontation.

Religious based conflicts usually mean conflict where religion is the excuse, the rallying cry, used by leaders to gain support for their particular cause. That cause can, and often is, a genuine sense of injustice in their community, but they feel that the only effective way to remedy that injustice is to associate the perceived enemy with a religious, or anti-religious, motivation. Once set in motion the larger community tends to split into opposing religious factions, with the individual people and families in each faction reluctantly, mostly out of fear of persecution by their own side, professing their support. Remove the cause – the perceived injustice maybe – but how to remove the generations of inbuilt prejudice?

We do not need to look just at racial or religious intolerance to see this process in action. We only have to look for example at some of the more extreme elements that pretend to be football supporters. Both sides look for conflict as a means of satisfying their need for a unifying cause. And this aspect might be due to another gene altogether. The need to belong, to be part of a group, to feel secure in an insecure world, in the knowledge that help is always at hand. So sometimes there is an instinctive need to invent a threat, perhaps by magnifying a minor incident, in order to command attention from the rest of the peer group. Once set in motion, with rational judgement often impaired by alcohol, the resulting conflict is hard to stop.

Another factor, though perhaps when it happens is only a short term event, is a kind of fleeting insanity which sometimes affects excited groups or crowds. This most ugly manifestation can be seen in rampaging mobs. They may be so called football supporters or striking workers. They could equally be groups of Iraqis celebrating the murders of US soldiers. This frightening temporary surge of crowd emotion is remarkably similar whatever the adopted cause. The participants temporarily lose control of themselves and commit horrifying violent acts against people and property. But could this possibly be another example of some kind of collective Id taking control of the crowd, in the same way as, in chapter 2, we contemplated its manifestation in the unified behaviour of a flock of birds, or in a shoal of fish, where no single bird or fish appeared to be their leader?

So the evil gene repeatedly re-asserts itself. The protagonists don't want to stop fighting. If they did stop then all their own failings and lack of achievement, which they have been blaming on each other, would have to find an explanation within their own camps. The perceived enemy would no longer be there to provide the excuse, the unifying threat, and a cause for the rallying cry.

From our comparatively settled part of the world, could we expose this unwanted part of our genetic inheritance, to those who see only threats in each other, as presenting the greater challenge to their existence. If only they could see that the real threat lay in these genes which are rooted, like a disease, in the whole human race, setting group against group, nation against nation. Here would be a totally external threat, like an invasion from outer space, where everyone could become united against it.

There is of course, another quite independent source of conflict. Greed, and the crime which it breeds, both local and international, which produces wealth for the criminals and poverty and suffering for the victims. In this case no amount of unifying gene theory will take away the bitterness felt by the victims, and if no legal redress is in prospect, can we condemn them for taking matters into their own hands and fighting back?

But crime is often simply the product of envy. Consider any community where perhaps the majority of a population are living reasonably comfortable lifestyles with all the visible trappings, such as good housing, new cars and other luxury equipment. We have to recognise that there may be some in that community who have, often through no fault of their own, failed to achieve sufficient income to enable them to enjoy those rewards, and see no hope of ever acquiring them in their lifetime. It is not difficult to understand their temptation to try to get started on the ladder of prosperity by embarking on a criminal course. It is not enough just to condemn their actions. They are to some extent a product of our unfair society and we need to look for possible causes in our own social and political environment.

Add to that the political opportunists, overpopulation, and economic migrants. Entrepreneurial dominance breeding resentment in those who would otherwise be content to stay as they were. Consider the leaders and those who blindly follow. And the arms manufacturers – those who use guns should realise that every time they fire a bullet they are swelling the coffers of the arms manufacturers and suppliers, and the coffers of those who invest in them.

So where do we look for solutions. We could consider the more 'police state' or communist style of government, but has that not been tried and failed? Power to control the excesses of a few to protect the many seems worth having, but power can also lead to corruption as some of those in control begin to 'feather their own nests'. It seems we have nowhere to turn for a solution.

Consider conflict deliberately created to exploit differences between ethnic, religious or disadvantaged subdivisions of a country's population in order to benefit e.g.. arms manufacturers or to weaken its economy.

But is it always a deliberately contrived exploitation?. Perhaps it is instead a cumulative effect of many smaller entrepreneurial activities, and some criminal involvement, which ultimately becomes self perpetuating, and unstoppable except by major conflict. In this case the religious or ethnic components simply become caught up in the conflict, because each is affected differently due to their varying degrees of economic success.

This does not exclude the involvement of arms manufacturers. They are always ready and willing to provide the weaponry. And since both sides in a dispute are sometimes supported by ideologically opposing major powers, the latter can then find themselves each trying to ensure that their supply of arms at least balances that of the other side. And external support for a particular side in a dispute is sometimes dependent on their prior commitment to buy weaponry, with little regard for the resulting degree of poverty which their populations would then have to endure.

In some countries there is a very long history of religious or ethnic based divisions which have become deeply entrenched in their collective psyche. Even if the bulk of a populace have become sufficiently intelligent to disregard their historic differences it requires only a few individuals to keep the conflict alive. And sometimes even these few realise that the historic reasons have become irrelevant but nonetheless continue to exploit them for their own personal gain. Also of course, in any country with poverty and unemployment many of those who join illegal armed groups do so because it is often the only way to earn money and to benefit from commandeered scarce food supplies.

The roots of conflict seem to lay in the most basic origins of animal life. It is to our great discredit that many in the human race have not yet emerged from that primitive condition and continue to respond to largely irrational fears about the aggressive intentions of each other. But some conflict is also generated by the efforts of those who try to suppress the inbred characteristics of different races and creeds. It is surely vital that these differences are instead broadcast loud and clear so that each can recognise the other's needs and respect their points of view. It is also necessary that each comes to realise the impact that their lifestyles have on each other and, where necessary, exercise some restraint. If a particular race's habits or activities are offensive to another we should not expect the offended party to suddenly learn to enjoy it, and the offenders should realise this. This is relevant in urban as well as international situations.

Urban conflict is sadly but all too frequently caused when a small incident, perhaps involving two individuals of different race, is interpreted by many in their respective communities as representing an attack on all of them. It is probable that in time the majority of people would learn to live happily in multi-racial communities if it were not for the excesses of a few.

International conflict though, owes much more to the multiplicity of vested interests which individual governments have supported in order to gain power. Threats to those interests, both internal and external, often cause those in power to stimulate, and subsequently exaggerate, threats from abroad in order to maintain a delicate balance between the extremes of their own supporting factions.

For this reason they often need to adopt aggressive postures and we should learn to 'read between the lines' to realise that other countries' condemnation is sometimes carefully calculated to give internal support to those leaders. Recognition of these factors, and even more analysis and publicising of the real issues in any threatening situation, are needed if we are to avoid being dragged into yet more unnecessary conflicts.

Sometimes of course it is necessary for some of the more stable nations to restrain a particular country's leaders who have become unstable and unresponsive to rational debate, dragging their whole population into aggression. Innocent and unwilling peoples have to suffer the retribution of their neighbours because they dare not criticise their own tyrannical government. But here again there are often many grey areas where the collective desire to help is hampered by powerful vested interests, both industrial and political, which tend to take precedence over purely humane considerations.

How can we ever extricate ourselves from this appalling mess? Certainly the United Nations in principle is moving in the right direction, but it can easily lose its credibility if one or more nations decide to ignore its collective judgement whenever they disagree with it. The United States has on several occasions, without a clear UN mandate, intervened in another country when it considers it to be a threat to World peace and, as in Vietnam, has come to regret it afterwards. Its intervention in Iraq, again with questionable motives and debatable UN justification, has shown similar signs of belated second thoughts.

And hanging like the Sword of Damoclese over all of us on this planet is the awful risk of Nuclear Armageddon. All the time some of the stronger nations have a nuclear weapon capability many others will feel threatened – not always directly from those weapons perhaps, but certainly from a general lack of bargaining power in international negotiations. And as each seeks to achieve a similar 'status' their immediate neighbours feel threatened and themselves seek the same capability. It is hard to see how we can collectively extricate ourselves from this threat, but at the very least those nations with nuclear weapons should avoid using their assumed superiority to intervene in the affairs of others.

And the World's armaments industries need international control as well. All the time powerful financial interests stand to gain from conflict millions of innocent people will continue to suffer. And before we end these thoughts on vested interests are we so sure that some of us don't unwittingly benefit financially from weapons production? How many of us know whether our own investments, or even our bank accounts, might benefit from such financial dealings, and even if we did how could we ever separate our own country's essential defence needs from the production of arms for other countries?

And always, lurking in the background, are the criminal elements, ready to take advantage of a country's instability in order to profit by financial transactions, arms sales, drugs etc. Also the 'Nazi' style militants – a threat from a history which they try to deny, already active in some parts.

In recent years I have become increasingly concerned at what seems to me to be a possible course of events for my own country – the UK, in which the proportion of the non-ethnic population could one day reach a critical level where inter- racial conflict becomes difficult to avoid.

Recent history is full of comparable examples, and the

pattern is usually the same or similar. It starts with a small intake of immigrants who settle in and are easily accepted as part of the community. But three factors then develop to destabilise it. First the numbers of immigrants increase either from new intake or from their high birth rates. Next there is an increase in immigrant entrepreneurial activity leading to a financial success rate exceeding that of many in the indigenous population. It is of course inevitable that many immigrants who have the enterprise to emigrate in the first place are those who have entrepreneurial capabilities. Finally there arises a disaffected, initially small, part of the indigenous population who, due to their own lack of success, become increasingly resentful of the immigrants success rate and who, rather than face up to their own inadequacies, start to blame the immigrants for their own failings.

It is only a small step from there to arrive at mob violence and ultimately to a stage where both communities feel threatened by each other. The apparently inevitable escalation leads to popular support for, and election of, extremist anti-immigrant governments, who then transform into dictatorships. The so called immigrant population, often resident for several generations, then suffer various degrees of persecution even to the extent of being forced to re-emigrate to a country which was assumed to be their ancestral home.

Uganda was a good example of this, where, as I said earlier, Idi Amin became popular due to the unwelcome success of the immigrant population, mostly from India, the latter being ejected from their homes and sent either back to an India which most of them had never known, or to any other country that would accept them.

But as far as our own country (the UK) is concerned we, along with several other European nations, have to face up to our own past. We, over recent centuries, have emigrated to, and sometimes invaded, and taken over, many other countries all over the world, sometimes, as in the Americas, displacing or even largely eliminating their indigenous populations. Some guilt based recompense has since occurred as in Australia with the Aborigines, but in most cases the loss in irrecoverable.

So what can we do, now that we in the UK may be faced with the problem that the rest of the world is all too well acquainted with? We have no right to deny to others that which we ourselves have practiced in the past. Somehow we have to anticipate this evolution – educate from the earliest school days that there are differences of life style between races, not try to pretend they do not exist. Accept that those of us who have a much longer ancestry in the UK cannot easily adjust to accommodate the expectations of other races. Emphasise equality by all means, but do not deny our differences – instead broadcast them loud and clear – praising the good qualities and confining criticism only to individuals who deserve it rather than to their race as a whole.

We must acknowledge racial differences not deny them. We must allow all races to develop in their own way, but at the same time each must respect the other's sensitivities and especially recognise that generations of acquired life styles cannot be changed overnight. Some of our recent immigrants have come from countries where harsher conditions had conditioned them to adopt less honest ways in order to survive. It is not easy for them to change and adapt to life in a country where legally based systems are usually adequate. Perhaps it is time to create a Ministry of Inter-racial Affairs and raise the profile of this problem rather than try to pretend it does not exist, otherwise the UK will become yet one more trouble spot on this tormented planet. We have had more than enough warnings from our world's history. Time is running out.

At the time of writing this, comparatively new challenges to world stability are emerging. These are the increasing use of suicide bombers and hostage taking, both hard to combat because of their random and unpredictable nature, and because the victims are mostly innocent non-participants. But could those who commit such actions sometimes be justified, if in an otherwise helpless oppressed community they are prepared to sacrifice themselves as the only way to combat their strong militarised oppressors? This may seem an unacceptable view, but is it any different to the horrific actions we took in the 1939/45 war when both sides killed thousands of innocent civilians in massive air raids?

Some suicide bombers are of course unstable individuals, often belonging to militant groups with extreme fanatical religious motivations. But whatever the so called terrorists' reasons, those countries who feel under threat should at least be looking into their own world image, just in case their particular economic activities or military interventions are providing the very justification that the bombers, and the hostage takers, are seeking.

The saddest fact of all is that much of the major conflict in this world is caused by only a few militant people, and perhaps a few criminal elements, on one side or both, who persuade substantial elements of their populations that there is a threat from each other. The rest of us just want to get on with our lives.

So is there any way forward that could enable us to overcome all these difficulties and allow the human race to finally emerge into the light of reason from the dark ages of conflict, which have already lasted thousands of years. Or will the human race continue, for century after century, squabbling over everything, with the greatest prize of all awaiting them when they stop – peace and huge advances in living quality for all of us?

But there is another factor which we have yet to address. How can we ever be sure when judging each other as being innocent or guilty, or as good or evil, when our judgement could be unknowingly influenced by our own inherited, but possibly flawed, thinking processes?

16. INNOCENCE AND GUILT

Are we all victims of our own ignorance?

If we are ever to fully understand the origins and causes of conflict there is one further essential factor that has to be acknowledged.

All of us in the human race must sooner or later concede that our thinking processes may be flawed – that whatever the subject of our judgement our logic may be unconsciously biassed, or is at least inadequate (and the author of this book is no exception). We each inherit a subconscious brain structure that can predispose us towards a certain way of thinking. It is for instance no good simply blaming the various religious extremists for believing that they each represent the only true way. Their causes are pursued with great dedication. It is hard wired into their brains. Jewish leaders for example, believe they have the right to rule half of Palestine – while many Palestinians try to defend themselves against what they, rightly or wrongly, regard as an illegal occupying force. Both sides' beliefs may be substantially inherited and are sincerely practised.

Somehow, even when acknowledging the natural processes which have ensured the survival of the physically and mentally fittest, we have come to regard each of us as being consciously and deliberately responsible for our behaviour towards each other. We have mostly failed to recognise that our mental or intellectual capability may not be totally under our voluntary control.

When we each emerged into the world from our mothers' wombs we were already equipped with a certain amount of pre-programmed brain structure, and this structure, although we had no awareness of it, inevitably came to affect our subsequent judgement.

At first we accept most of our inherited characteristics, and early parental guidance, without question, although at a later stage we might find that certain of our parents' attitudes or criticisms cause us to rebel and take opposite views. But probably that very act of rebelling has again made use of part of our inherited brain structure, even though that part may have bypassed one or more generations and have been influenced by ancestors existing long before our own parents.

And in the same way that the reproductive process is supposed to ensure the dominance of superior genes, that process could also mean that earlier ancestral conflict might have contributed towards our ability to express preferences, even to the extent of disobedience.

So, as I said in chapter four, is there any stage at which we could detach ourselves from having an unavoidable subconsciously influenced response to our daily encounters with each other and with our environment?

The answer has to be partially 'Yes'. If our inherited views have included a component that has allowed us to ask questions and become receptive to some degree of morally, or even immorally, inspired teaching, and that taught view is seen as being more acceptable to us than that which we already held, then we could be said, in that case at least, to have succeeded in changing ourselves. But we might still find some subtle elements of our original thinking processes intruding, especially when we are in some unexpected stressful situation. And short of total brainwashing it is unlikely that we could ever replace all our inherited characteristics, even if we wanted to.

What therefore does this mean when we are trying to assess the guilt of an individual for what we perceive to be their misdeeds? Can we simply excuse them on the grounds that they were helpless victims of their own inherited brain structure? And is our own judgement, or even trial by jury, also suspect for the same reasons?

Obviously in the case of serious crime of a kind that affects the welfare of others in a community, that community has to protect itself from its repetition. But if on the other hand that assumed criminal has suffered from the collective unjust oppression of his community then again we find ourselves with questionable judgement.

Then we come to the question of greed. This is surely yet another inherited 'survival of the fittest' instinct. So what right have we to criticise its appearance in each other if we have no mechanism for eliminating it from our natural make up?

Here enters conflict, and the collective effort of communities at local, national and international level, each to argue their side of the case. Once again we find ourselves at the mercy of partially inherited and substantially unreliable human reasoning processes. Plus of course the need of those negotiators to respond to the multiplicity of often questionable views of those they are trying to represent.

Is it possible that an assembly of a large number of us, at least of those collectively regarded as having a good measure of intellect, could develop an agreed formula for expressing totally unbiased judgement? Surely if enough of us are involved we could be reasonably confident of producing an intellectual elite completely free of irrational bias. Democracy was supposed to achieve that of course, but even the most intellectually equiped democrats have to please their supporters.

We do not, and probably never will have, a totally independent and unbiased adjudicator, capable of acquiring and encompassing all knowledge of a given situation. And even if we had, or could rely on the UN to perform that role, it is another matter altogether to persuade the conflicting factions to accept that authority's judgement?

Perhaps this is the point where we should turn once more to the computer. Create our own electronic version of God? Progressively feed into that super machine all aspects of every known conflicting view and program it to give us a final perfectly unbiased judgement. But what happens when our own subconsciously biased human brains cannot accept the result? As the Christian Bible quotes of Jesus, 'let he who is without sin among you cast the first stone'.

In chapter seven, while expressing doubt about the existence of God in any of the forms depicted by most major religions, I conceded the possibility, or even probability, that some greater intelligent being might nonetheless exist, even though he, or it, seemed unable, or unwilling, to intervene. But could we draw comparisons with our own remote observations of wild nature. For those of us who on occasion look at television programs on that subject there have been opportunities recently where powerful telescopic camera lens have enabled us to watch the most intimate interactions of various animals without them being in any way aware that their activities were being recorded.

In those observations the photographers have usually made it a rule never to intervene, even when they see wild creatures attacking and killing each other, on the grounds that they would be interfering in natural processes.

So perhaps we in turn are being watched by beings superior to ourselves, able to use even more sophisticated apparatus than we can understand, who are similarly restrained from helping us? 'More wild thinking' you might say, but surely, considering all the other inexplicable phenomena of this world, (*see chapter 6*) we cannot exclude this possibility altogether.

Could that thought at least give some of those who lack moral inhibitions in their daily lives, due to having no faith in a more conventional god, some cause to reconsider the morality of their actions, and even to contemplate being called to account on some future day of judgement. And that judgement might be a more reliable version than we humans can exercise.

Much conflict arises only because neither side has total grasp of all relevant factors, or even attaches equal importance to those they recognise. So unless we can find some way to be totally sure of correctly judging guilt or innocence, even in ourselves, and all the time even the most dedicated leaders are constrained by the inadequate judgement of those they are trying to represent, an end to perpetual conflict would seem to be as remote as ever.

So we are left with what appears to be an unsolvable situation in which all humans are, in varying degrees, innocent victims of their own inadequate reasoning capabilities. If only it were possible that all conflicting factions could be made aware that their judgement might be at fault. But even those who claim religious justification for their aggression are unlikely to find such cautionary teachings in the main religious disciplines, even if they took the trouble to look for them. And other subconscious motivations often intrude to take over their reasoning.

But is there another way forward? What of the more positive activities of mankind? Shining through all this conflict there is, in spite of all the setbacks, an irrepressible urge to be creative – to design and build – to invent machines to do our work – to find cures for diseases – to compose music and practise the arts. If these activities could contribute to a better world for every nation, might they finally divert all mankind, innocent or guilty, from these senseless confrontations? Perhaps we could gain some comfort, and hope for the future, from contemplating our achievements?

17. HUMAN ACHIEVEMENTS

Looking on the bright side

If the presence of human life in this world had to be justified solely in terms of our contribution to the global environment, we might be found way down on the scale of one to ten. But if some visitor from another world were, on seeing our planet for the first time, to report back to his own world on any signs of civilisation, he would probably begin by commenting on our major structures. Our cities, especially those with tall buildings and bridges – our modes of transport with trains and aircraft and giant ships. And then, as he came closer, seeing the greater detail – the roads with their streaming vehicles – their human inhabitants, moving in all directions – sometimes gathering – sometimes dispersing, he might wonder what purpose kept them all in motion.

Our visitor might then, if he could infiltrate into the midst of us without being noticed, become increasingly intrigued by all the devices we have invented to sustain ourselves – our heated or air conditioned homes – our domestic appliances – our communication systems and our entertainment equipment – though some of the latter items might cause him to doubt our sanity.

Moving on to our scientific achievements, he would encounter great advances in medicine, agriculture, food distribution, power and energy supply systems. He might find out, perhaps with some slight apprehension, about our recent successes in exploring the space near our planet, and wonder how long it would be before we succeeded in travelling further afield.

He might also note – with understandable consternation, our development of the most terrible weapons, and begin to question our long term prospects for survival, especially when he realised the extent to which we were still at risk from international conflict.

For the arts – music, dance, graphical representation – his appreciation would of course depend on his own world's modes of expression. But our literature, assuming his advanced civilization enabled him to interpret it, and to select the best, could surely evoke some praise.

As far as our contemporary vision allows, we appear to have made incredible progress in understanding our world and in equipping ourselves, or a least some of us, with multiple comforts, intellectual opportunities and recreational facilities. We must be proud of it all, but keeping in mind that much of humanity yet remains to benefit from it. And be sad that some of our efforts have been wasted in conflict.

So our extra terrestrial visitor, who has come to assess whether the human race qualifies to be accepted in his club of planetary civilizations, would probably give a guarded report and say that we have certainly made tremendous advances, but as far as membership is concerned – perhaps not yet.

Looked at in isolation though, our achievements like architecture and engineering ought surely to get some credit. The urge to create massive structures that are both pleasing to the eye and of sound construction has been with us since primitive man first started to build stone shelters. But it was essentially the development of temple building and royal palace construction that brought about the evolution of architecture and to some extent the early engineering principles on which it depended. But whereas architecture, like the various art forms, can please or displease according to the perceptions of the beholder, engineering has the very strict discipline of functional efficiency. It can be modified to accommodate architectural demands but only at the risk of complicating its prime purpose. The fact that a piece of machinery or other engineering structure is sometimes also aesthetically pleasing, merely demonstrates what I said previously about animal beauty and its relationship with strength and economy.

Our ability in the past couple of centuries to harness many of the planet's energy resources has of course led to a massive expansion in engineering projects, but today's structures are mostly not built to last more than a few hundred years. The vast hydroelectric dams and shipping canals might last a little longer, but the great steel suspension bridges for example, if left without maintenance for even a hundred years would probably not survive. So if our particular civilisation were to disappear it is unlikely that there would be much left, at least in architectural or engineering achievement, to mark our time on Earth.

But the sheer spatial perception involved in modern human creations means that mankind has attained another dimension altogether in his quest for self expression. The spectacular and occasionally attractive buildings that dominate our cities; the huge and undoubtedly beautiful airliners, and the massive ships, not all of them beautiful, that now convey us and our cargoes about the globe, represent only the beginning of our expanding vision. The only restraint it seems is financial, and this is especially evident in the present frustrations of those scientists and engineers who have the knowledge, but not the resources, for further space exploration.

Most of these, sometimes extravagant, achievements have brought many rewards, although not without a measure of tragedy and damage to the environment as well.

But regardless of any doubts about the benefits of all these discoveries, there is no way in which we could have avoided making them. They were there for us to find and use, and the human animal could not avoid having an enquiring mind. The need of many of us to create machines and structures seems to stem from a desire to extend our own personalities, to have power and influence beyond that normally available to us. Only future generations, if there are any, will be able to judge whether the overall quality of life has been consequently enhanced for all mankind, or only for those of us who were the first to get possession of those resources.

The arts, on the other hand, if we exclude architecture, largely function without the restraints of practical applicability. They are there for the artists to indulge in free expression, to produce, whether it be music or theatre or dance, or sculpture or graphical interpretation, their particular visions of the world about them. And regardless of the degree of appreciation which their works attract, even the most critical of us surely cannot fail to concede that overall they represent some of our greatest intellectual achievements. They express and interpret human emotions in ways not available to ordinary language.

Medicine also deserves to be high on our credit list, although it could be said that much of it has evolved to treat conditions brought about by some of our own unnatural modes of living, including high population densities. Diseases like AIDS are probably simply nature's way of responding to overcrowding, and finding a cure may, if we ignore our natural compassion for the victims, just be seen as adding to the problem. But our most important advance has to be the incredible unravelling of nature's DNA structure. Here we have a chance to understand and possibly treat every known malady.

One serious challenge though is increasingly emerging

from the remarkable ability of some disease bacteria to develop resistance to antibiotics. We may even find this foe to be our ultimate Armageddon, and lose.

As for communications, almost every new year seems to bring fresh advances, though some of them could be regarded as luxuries rather than necessities. We now have the ability to contact each other almost instantly wherever we are on the planet, and to choose from dozens of television and radio programmes. And many of us can now have rapid access to a world-wide library of information on almost any known subject. We can also communicate far beyond the confines of our planet, not just to astronauts on the moon, but even to unmanned craft beyond the solar system. Another incredible area of progress is our increasing ability to receive and interpret radio emissions and visual data from remote parts of the universe, albeit with the recognition that much of it can be millions of years old by the time it reaches us.

We should also praise those members of the human race who, voluntarily and tirelessly, and sometimes at great risk, are trying to help the disadvantaged peoples of the world. Hopefully these groups and organisations will continue to expand, and become powerful enough to bring more and more pressure to bear on wealthier countries' governments to solve the problems of the underprivileged.

So with all these great achievements to our credit it seems that the only factor holding us back from emerging into a benign and beautiful world is our collective insufficiency of intelligence when it comes to making good use of them. We view with despair the intolerance and greed which repeatedly undermine all our efforts to make progress, especially when it comes to providing economic help to poorer countries. And even for the wealthier nations, economic success has not always improved the quality of life for all their people. Let us hope that those who try to help will somehow win through, but nature itself will not tolerate much more messing about.

What can we do, if anything, to ensure a better future?

18. THE FUTURE

Where do we go from here?

Can we approach the future with any clear sense of direction? I think the very least we can do is to draw up some kind of list of ideals and then assess both the degree to which we fall short on each and the practical difficulties of achieving them.

A possible list could be:-

a) Peaceful resolution of religious and racially based conflicts

b) Universal acceptance of human rights

c) World wide fair trading

d) Reaffirmation of moral values through education

e) Conservation of our planet's resources

f) Reduction in pollution to minimise global warming

In each of these ideals the three main factors preventing progress are vested interests, dishonesty, and a natural instinct for survival which makes most successful humans reluctant to seek any change in their current life style or ways of doing business. But we also have to take into account the inability of perhaps a majority of humans to understand the economic and practical complexities involved. Whole populations can be easily persuaded for or against a particular course of action by over-simplified presentation of facts – quite often propounded by leaders who themselves have failed to understand fully what they are doing, or at least are driven by their need to maintain support from other activists with less democratic motivation.

The resolution of most conflicts based on religious and inter-racial differences can only come about by dialogue, but while there has been much understanding at the highest levels, it is the perception of the peoples as a whole which has been difficult to change. We need an overriding discipline, some creed which can reflect beliefs common to all the major religious groups. If we look at the roots of most religions, their basic message is justice, at least of a kind which is believed to meet the approval of God. Could we extract from each of them their core beliefs, and bring them together as some kind of universal morality? But even if this were possible, another perhaps much greater hurdle to overcome is the way in which many religions have become associated with past conflicts – leaving a bitter harvest of recriminations. Even so, we must continue trying to bring understanding, and a universal moral code may help – it could be the only way forward. (*see also Chapter 11*).

It would be wonderful if the current almost universally professed recognition of human rights was consistently adopted in practise. We have moved quite a way forward on this, with a clear UN declaration and apparent international consensus, but legal interpretation has allowed some countries to ignore human rights on professed national security grounds. How do we address such issues short of war or the blunt instrument of trade embargoes?

There are still many parts of the world where there is torture and imprisonment without a fair trial, but the issues are often very complex, and where a particular government is itself insecure then internal repression can result. Here though government instability is often associated with poor economic performance and the better off countries should be more concerned with improved trading opportunities so that the offending state can be persuaded to dispense with internal repressive measures.

Poverty often breeds crime and conflict, which in turn

breed extreme governments, although sometimes small countries can be potentially wealthy with huge natural resources, especially mineral wealth, but benefitting only those in power while their populace still remain in poverty. Here we need to trade with care, if possible imposing conditions that ensure more even distribution of that wealth.

So perhaps everything can be resolved by fair trading. Sounds all right in principle, but how to start? As with the efforts to give financial support to poor countries, this too is held back by powerful vested interests, especially by those whose trade is supplemented by agricultural subsidies. But if removing those subsidies succeeds only in persuading some farmers to give up agriculture then we become less able to supply other countries at competitive prices. So the contradictions are all too evident, with poorer countries' exports failing to compete against subsidised exports from the better off. There has to be a compromise sooner or later. Poor countries tend to breed aggressive leaders, and the resources we waste in conflict with them would be better spent in helping their populations to prosper.

And all the time we have multiple currencies in the world there have to be complex systems of exchange rates, each reflecting a particular country's current degree of prosperity. I am reminded of a system which has been practised for many years by our own UK government, in which a process of equalisation grants takes account of the relative prosperity of each county – allocating central government finance in favour of poorer authorities. There is a similar process functioning in the European Union and in its early stages of development in the UN, all aimed at helping those countries with geographic limitations to their ability to improve their own economic performance. Some charities are also trying to help. But complex restraints such as perceived poor internal control of distribution often hold back other countries from committing themselves. We have a long way to go but it is the only way to enable fair trading to become feasible, and in world prosperity terms it is bound to cost less than the burden of conflict.

Problem solved? partially perhaps, but fair trading also has to take account of the welfare of our planet, our only lifeboat, and with no hope at present of us finding any other home. Trade which involves consuming non-renewable mineral resources – in effect burning the fixtures and fittings of our only source of life support – has to stop. The oil rich nations will, at present rate, ultimately become the oil poor. So we must develop trade instead primarily in food and other renewable resources, ensuring that fuel consuming distribution and other energy waste is minimised.

We also have to take account of criminal activities. How can we ever hope to combat crime without drifting into a kind of 'police state', which has its own associated risks?

And even if we succeed in evening out the distribution of wealth and dealing with the estimated 800 million or so of the world's population who are currently known to be undernourished, there still remains the task of improving and maintaining the quality of life for everyone. That to some extent means better education, but it also means coming to terms with the restraints on more natural physical and recreational activities that result from living in large congested cities. Limitations on outdoor pursuits produce an inward looking community that finds itself having to rely increasingly on artificial entertainment, including television, where a constant diet of criminal and confrontational domestic scenarios is acted out with maximum emphasis on senseless violence and sex, consequently training our children to believe that such activities are a normal part of life.

Another growing development has been the increase in mindless vandalism. It is not sufficient to simply blame the culprits. Here again, if their natural instinct for adventure is constrained by dense urban environments, and we continue to educate them by portraying violent destruction on television drama, night after night, it is our so called civilisation that must take responsibility.

The outcome of all these deliberations must inevitably lead to the need to reaffirm moral values, otherwise all human achievement will be just a hollow victory over the material world's challenges, with no overall values to ensure that progress is matched by such qualities as kindness, tolerance and care for each other.

Conservation of our planet's finite resources must go hand in hand with our efforts to reduce pollution and to combat global warming. The awful truth is belatedly beginning to dawn on even the most doubting of world governments. It may already be too late to prevent a serious world temperature rise, with all its implications of flooding, displaced populations and mass starvation. Nonetheless we must do everything possible to try to limit its effects.

But so far we have looked only at the immediate future. There is another, much more distant future to contemplate. In chapter 12 I referred to our tendency to look at the past in terms of only a few thousand years, rather than contemplate the millions of years of our evolution. Similarly we should open up our minds to the vastly greater future and try to envisage life which might exist in hundreds of thousands of years from now, or even maybe tens of millions of years. What could evolve say, after the next ice age? Would there still be creatures like ourselves? Or would all traces of our human form have disappeared.

Much could depend on whether today's humans become sufficiently intelligent, or even collectively concerned enough, to plan not just for the next few hundred years, as we do now to some extent, but to look to a time when our planet might become uninhabitable for life as we currently enjoy it.

Should we humans, the only present tenants of this planet who appear to have sufficient reasoning powers, be assuming responsibility for our planet's future by anticipating and trying to prevent possible natural global disasters? If enough resources became available for research, could we for example find a way to divert an incoming asteroid, or modify or even prevent another ice age.

Or should our present human race be content to carry on satisfying only today's needs, or at most responding just to perceived imminent crises, and ignore vital but more remote foreseeable hazards, until tomorrow's people awake one day to find it is too late?

19. CONCLUSION

The beginning of tomorrow's world

In this brief look at Life I hope I have gone some way towards expressing my view of this incredible situation, in which we all find ourselves, trapped in bodies we did not choose, on our tiny isolated planet, without any instruction manual, left to get on with things as best we can.

In the preceding chapters I have attempted to find an explanation for the mysterious quality we call life, in its many forms. In considering that incredible apparatus the human brain, I have tried to identify the nature of consciousness and its dwelling place, and above all to locate the Id – the inner self – the spectator – that uses that consciousness to observe the world and make decisions.

I have sought help from the writings of scientists and philosophers who, in their endless search for answers have explored one direction after another, often coming up with apparently major discoveries about the way things appear to operate, only to find that their way is blocked when they ask the final question why. 'That is enough' the keeper of the door of ultimate knowledge appears to say – 'the key is not for you'.

And looking at the evolution of religions, with each claiming to represent the only true way, I have wondered if those beliefs, especially where they are used as an excuse for conflict, might even be holding us back from emerging into a more enlightened world. But for those who already doubt the existence of conventionally depicted gods, I have not excluded the possibility of some undetectable superior intelligent beings watching over us, who no more interfere in our conflicts and natural disasters than we do when observing much of wild nature.

For the future, I have considered the many factors that we need to address for our long term survival, both economic and in our relationships with each other, and also with our fragile home planet which, due either to our own activities or to natural disaster, might even one day be no longer habitable.

Life is the phenomenon which we all possess, yet none of us understand. We participate in an eternal process of human advancement being repeatedly set back by conflict, good against evil, and all enacted on a stage where the structure is on very insecure foundations indeed. But assuming our planet remains habitable, a brighter future might even yet be possible for everyone, if only we can make use of the more beneficial scientific discoveries and overcome the evil aspects of human nature which divide us all. Otherwise all our efforts will count for nothing in the annals of eternity.

And if we try to look beyond the confines of our tiny world with all its petty squabbles, there could yet be a far greater stage for us to play on. It is inconceivable that life, whatever its mysterious origins, has occurred only on our planet. Already some of our radio output will have reached far into our galaxy and betrayed our presence.

So one day we may be called upon to overcome our own collective introspections and present a united front to other worlds and to other life forms in the universe, some with intelligence levels far superior to our own. Perhaps that is what we all need to bring us to our senses. We would do well to anticipate that event and put our own house in order before they arrive.

THE WINDS OF TIME

I stood in the doorway of time past,
And listened to the night wind,
Conversing with the late summer trees,
Telling of its journey through eternity and of its destination,
Far beyond any future I could possibly imagine.

Was there an end to time I asked,
But the wind had gone on its way without answering.
Perhaps when it comes again,
To take the autumn leaves,
I will go with them.

INDEX

A
aboriginal tribes 75
Aborigines 110
Abraham 60
after death 11
agnosticism 65
ancestors' experiences 26
Andromeda 46
arms manufacturers 105
assessment of guilt 115
atheism 65

B
basic moral concepts 70
basic reproductive process 7
biochemical 47
biological selection process 38
birth control 91
brain – electrochemical impulses 12
brain – pre-programmed structure 114

C
Carbon dioxide 81, 90
child labour 83
Christ 60, 69
collective Id 9,103
Communism 67

complex network of services 92
composition of matter 40
conflicts ongoing in the World 96
Consciousness
    definition 9
    emotions 24
    harmonic structure 21
    human 10
    music 20
    processing functions 21
    sounds and sights 20
    The inner self 29
    the subconscious 29
cosmic identity 73
creative arts 3

D

Darwinism 38
defective genes 87
defining consciousness 9
definition of intelligence 88
Deism 56, 57, 65, 66
dense urban environments 129
digital photography 47
DNA molecular mechanisms 35, 47

E

Earth as our only lifeboat 72
Einstein 41
Einstein's relativity theories 40
electric vehicles 84
electrochemical 47
electromagnetic phenomena 40
electromagnetic spectrum 46
evolution theory 38

evolutionary processes 32
existence of God 50
extinct civilizations 4

F
fair trading 125
flawed thinking processes 113
fossilized remains 75
Frank Buchman 70
free will 59
frightening phenomena 51, 52
fuel cells 82
fuel taxes 84

G
gamma and cosmic rays 46
general anaesthetic 39
global warming 80
graphic arts 22
gravitation 40

H
habitable areas 81
hostage taking 111
Human brain
- automatic reflexes 16
- cerebral cortex 20
- co-ordinating centre 16
- control centre 19
- electromagnetic interference 13
- equivalent of 17
- inner sanctum 16
- The Id 9, 12, 16, 103
- the inner person 16

human genome project 35, 47

I
Ignorance, innocent victims of their own 117
infinite universe 64
infinity and eternity 74
infrared 46
inner self – the spectator 131
invisible activity 12
Iraq 108
Islam 60
Islamic internal conflict 98
Israeli / Palestinian conflict 98

K
Kindness and compassion 88

L
legacy of bitterness 102
life's various forms 7

M
magnetic fields 12
major volcanic eruption 93
Marxism 68
Maxwell 41
mindless vandalism 129
Morality
    moral code 54, 60
    moral common ground 70
    moral ethics 68
    Moral Re-Armament Organisation 70
    moral values 129
    morality 67
    morally appropriate cost 83
Moses 60
Muhammad 60

mystery about our existence 64

N
natural evolution 33
Nature's creative capability 35
Newton 41
Noah's Ark 38
Northern Ireland 98
Nuclear Armageddon 108

O
oil rich nations 128
open-mindedness 49
other frequencies 46
oxygen depletion 82

P
Paganism 70
       and pantheism 65
Palestine 100, 118
Particle accelerator at CERN 44
persecution of the Jews 99
personality 11, 25
planet's resources 80
planet's rotation 3
planetary environment 84
planetary hypothesis 3
pollution 80, 93
population control 91
potential disaster 33
prehistoric inbuilt survival instincts 101
pre-programmed brain structure 114-116
primitive evolution 87
procreation process 89

R

racial intolerance 2, 110
radio 12
rational judgements 96
rational scientific explanations 63
reasoning processes 10
religious constraints 37
religious doctrines 2
reproduction 35
reproductive process 87
resistance to antibiotics 123
responsibility for behaviour 113
retrogressive evolution 34
roots of conflict 106
Rwanda 100

S

scientific achievements 119
secular alternatives to religion 70
self awareness 11, 19, 26
self correction 114
solar system 2
static electricity 41
subconscious brain structure 113
Sudan 101
suffering 61, 67
suicide bombers 111
Sunni and Shi'ite 98
Sunni and Shi'ite divisions of Islam 69
superior intelligent beings 50, 116, 132
survival of the fittest 87, 89
sword of Damoclese 108

T

television 12

Thomas Paine 65
Transmissions
    gravity 12
    light 41-42
    magnetic fields 12
    mobile phones 12, 49
    radio 12
    television 12

U
Uganda 99, 109,
ultimate knowledge 4,
ultraviolet 46
unbiased adjudicator 115
undetectable mediums 12
United Nations 107
universe 2
unreliable reasoning processes 115

V
video camera 16
Vietnam 107

W
wild nature 116
world of many religions 49
world's environment 33

X
X-rays 46

MORE DETAILED READING

The following books have done much to help me frame all those philosophical and scientific questions which I think still lack satisfactory answers.

Azimov's New Guide to Science *Isaac Azimov* Penguin

Big Questions in Science *Harriet Swain* Vintage

Brain Wise *Patricia Churchland* MIT Press

Dictionary of Contemporary World History *Jan Palmowski* Oxford

Dictionary of Religions *John R. Hinnells* Penguin

Encyclopaedia of Science *De Pre Axelrod* Wiley

Fire within the Eye *David Park* Princeton University Press

Galileo's Finger *Peter Atkins* Oxford

Magic Universe Nigel Calder   Oxford

Our Final Century *Martin Rees*   William Heinman

Philosophy Key Themes *Julian Baggini* Palgrave MacMillan

Physics and Philosophy *Werner Heisenberg* Penguin

QED The strange theory of light and matter *Richard P. Feynman* Penguin

Save The Earth *Jonathan Porritt* Dorling Kindersly

Science – A History *John Gribben* Penguin, Allen Lane

Steven Hawking- *Michael White, John Gribben* Penguin

The Age of Reason- *Thomas Paine* Citadel Press

The Astonishing Hypothesis- *Francis Crick* Simon and Schuster

The Book of Nothing- *John D. Barrow* Vintage

The Greenhouse Effect- *Stewart Boyle & John Ardill* New English Library

The Human Brain- *Susan Greenfield* Weidenfelt and Nicholson

The Human Genome- *Jeremy Cherfas* Dorling Kindersley

The Magic Furnace- *Marcus Chown* Vintage

Think- *Simon Blackburn* Oxford

What's it all about? *Julian Baggini* Granta